Frank Johnson Goodnow

Municipal Home Rule, a Study in Administration

Frank Johnson Goodnow

Municipal Home Rule, a Study in Administration

ISBN/EAN: 9783337158590

Printed in Europe, USA, Canada, Australia, Japan

Cover: Foto ©Lupo / pixelio.de

More available books at **www.hansebooks.com**

Municipal Home Rule

A Study in Administration

BY

FRANK J. GOODNOW, A.M., LL.B.

PROFESSOR OF ADMINISTRATIVE LAW IN COLUMBIA COLLEGE
AUTHOR OF "COMPARATIVE ADMINISTRATIVE LAW"

New York
THE MACMILLAN COMPANY
LONDON: MACMILLAN & CO., LTD.
1897

All rights reserved

PREFACE

The unsatisfactory character of American municipal government has, within the past few years, drawn unusual attention to the problems which it presents, and which, on account of the recent extraordinary development of municipal life, are becoming at the same time more numerous and more important. But as a result of the intimate connection of municipal with general government, all concrete attempts at municipal reform must of necessity depend upon an accurate delimitation of the sphere of action, which can, with due regard to the interests of the state as a whole, be assigned to our municipal organizations. The attempt to delimit such a sphere of action is the purpose of this little work. The science of municipal government in this country is, however, in such an early stage of development, and as a result, the theories with regard to municipal reform are so various, and indeed, so conflicting, that it has been thought wise to leave the realm of theories, based on *a priori* reasoning, and to endeavour in the delimitation of the sphere of municipal home rule, which it has been attempted to make, to find out exactly what is, by the present American law, the sphere of action of municipal corporations, which is recognized as local and *quasi* private, and in which, therefore, these bodies should move largely uncontrolled. The hope is entertained that this essay may be useful from both the legal and political points of view : from the legal point of view, because nowhere before has the attempt been made to collect and review either the cases decided by the courts relative to this matter, or the various constitutional provisions assuring to municipalities the right to manage their own affairs ; from the political point of view, because any theory which the courts may have formulated upon the subject has presumptions in its favour resulting from the fact that their conclusions have been reached through the following of inductive rather than deductive methods.

Acknowledgement is due to Professor John R. Cummons of the Indiana University for calling the author's attention to the recent development in the United States of a state supervision over the accounts of local corporations ; to Mr. Osgood Smith of the New York Bar for his assistance in going over the statutes bearing upon this point ; and to Mr. C. W. Tooke, Fellow in Columbia College, for the index and for several valuable suggestions.

FRANK J. GOODNOW.

COLUMBIA COLLEGE
IN THE CITY OF NEW YORK
April, 1895.

TABLE OF CASES CITED

	PAGE
Abercrombie v. Ely, 60 Mo. 23	215
Ah You, *Ex parte*, 82 Cal. 339	85
Alves' Executors v. Henderson, 16 B. Monroe, Ky. 131	211
Ashley v. The City of Port Huron, 35 Mich. 296	131
Astor v. The Mayor, 66 N. Y. 567	89
Atchison v. Bartholow, 4 Kans. 124	86
Augusta v. Perkins, 3 B. Monroe, Ky. 437	210
Bailey v. New York, 3 Hill, N. Y. 531	153
Barbier v. Connolly, 113 U. S. 27	38
Barnes v. District of Columbia, 91 U. S. 540	144
Barron v. Detroit, 94 Mich. 601	153
Beach v. Haynes, 12 Vt. 15	212
Beach v. Leahy, 11 Kans. 25	58
Beer Co. v. Massachusetts, 97 U. S. 659	38
Benson v. Mayor, 10 Barbour, N. Y. 223	200
Benton v. The Trustees of the Boston City Hospital, 140 Mass. 113	166
Bigelow v. Randolph, 15 Gray, 541	155, 160
Birmingham v. Rumsey, 63 Ala. 352	217
Bloomfield v. Charter Oak Bank, 121 U. S. 129	109
Bloomfield etc. Co. v. Calkins, 62 N. Y. 386	147
Board v. Reynolds, 44 Ind. 509	213
Board of Chosen Freeholders v. Buck, 51 N. J. Law, 155	79
Booth v. Woodbury, 32 Conn. 118	105
Borough of Dunmore's Appeal, 52 Pa. St. 374	28
Brenham, City of, v. German American Bank, 144 U. S. 173	51

	PAGE
Brewster v. Syracuse, 19 N. Y. 116	87
Briegel v. The City of Philadelphia, 135 Pa. St. 451	168
Britton v. Streber, 62 Mo. 370	87
Bronson v. Oberlin, 41 Ohio St. 476	67
Brooklyn Park Commissioners v. Armstrong, 45 N. Y. 234	212
Brown v. Atlanta, 66 Ga. 71	153
Brown v. Gates, 16 W. Va. 131	214
Bryant v. St. Paul, 33 Minn. 289	137
Burford v. Grand Rapids, 53 Mich. 98	126
Burrell v. Tacoma, 8 Wash. 156	199
Butler v. Pennsylvania, 10 How. U. S. 402	43
Buttrick v. The City of Lowell, 1 Allen, Mass. 172	134
Carr v. Northern Liberties, 35 Pa. St. 324	128
Carrington v. The City of St. Louis, 89 Mo. 208	172
Clark v. Cape May, 14 Atlantic Reporter, 581	77, 79
Clark et al. v. San Francisco, 134 U. S. 639	211
Clegg v. Richardson County, 8 Neb. 178	58
Clinton v. Cedar Rapids Railroad Co., 24 Iowa, 455	207
Clodfelter v. State, 86 N. C. 51	107
Cohen v. New York, 113 N. Y. 532	123
Commonwealth v. Patton, 88 Pa. St. 258	75, 79
Commonwealth v. Pittsburgh, 34 Pa. St. 496	28
Commonwealth v. Plaisted, 148 Mass. 375	85, 88
Commonwealth v. Tenny, 21 Ohio St. 499	147
Concord v. Robinson, 120 U. S. 165	104
Conrad v. Rogers, 70 Wis. 492	212
Council Grove, City of, 20 Kans. 619	74
Cowley v. Sunderland, 6 H. & N. 565	153
Coyle v. McIntire, 7 Houston, Del. 44	204
Crawfordsville, City of, v. Braden, 130 Ind. 149	47
Cullen, In the Matter of, 53 Hun, 534	27
Culver v. Streator, 130 Ill. 238	135
Curran v. Boston, 151 Mass. 505	139
Curtis v. Whipple, 24 Wis. 350	104

	PAGE
Darlington v. Mayor, 31 N. Y. 164	136, 185, 208
Dartmouth College v. Woodward, 4 Wheaton, 518	31, 40, 187
Davenport v. Peoria Ins. Co., 17 Iowa, 276	217
David v. Portland Water Coms., 14 Oregon, 98	199
Davies v. Los Angeles, 86 Cal. 37	85
Delahey v. Illinois, 2 Hill, N. Y. 162	180
Denton v. Jackson, 2 Johnson's Ch. 320	101
Denver v. Catelli, 4 Col. 25	131
Detroit v. Beckman, 34 Mich. 125	130
Devine v. Cook County, 84 Ill. 590	64, 86
Donovan v. The Board of Education, 85 N. Y. 117	165
Duanesburgh v. Jenkins, 57 N. Y. 177	52
Duke v. Rome, 20 Ga. 609	136
Dundy v. Richardson County, 8 Neb. 508	58
East Hartford v. Hartford Bridge Co., 10 How. 511	202
Eastman v. Meredith, 36 N. H. 296	151, 154
Edgerton v. The Third Municipality of New Orleans, 1 La. Ann. 435	214
Edwards v. The Town of Pocahontas, 47 Fed. Rep. 269	140
Eels v. Telephone Co., 143 N. Y. 133	147
Ellerman v. McMains, 30 La. Ann. 190	200
Essex Public Road Board v. Skinkle, 140 U. S. 304	208
Evansville v. State, 118 Ind. 426	88
Ex parte. See name of case.	
Fair v. Philadelphia, 88 Pa. St. 309	131
Fleishel v. Hightower, 62 Ga. 324	216
Ford v. Kendall School District, 121 Pa. St. 543	109
Forsyth v. Atlanta, 45 Ga. 152	123
Foster v. Fowler, 60 Pa. St. 27	216
Fowler v. Alexandria, 3 Peters, 398	136
Gage v. Graham, 57 Ill. 144	28
Galvin v. New York, 112 N. Y. 223	167
Garrard Co. Ct. v. Navigation Co., 10 Am. Law Reg. 151	104
Gibbons v. United States, 8 Wall. 269	107
Gilmore v. Norton, 10 Kans. 491	86

	PAGE
Girard v. Philadelphia, 7 Wall. 1	193
Gordon v. Cornes, 47 N. Y. 608	103
Gould v. The City of Topeka, 32 Kans. 485	132
Greencastle v. Martin, 74 Ind. 449	173
Grogan v. San Francisco, 18 Cal. 590	195
Guest v. Merion Water Co., 142 Pa. St. 610	216
Guilford v. Supervisors, 13 N. Y. 143	87
Haag v. Vanderburgh Co., 16 Ind. 511	155
Ham v. The Mayor, 70 N. Y. 459	165
Hand v. Brookline, 126 Mass. 324	158
Hannon v. St. Louis Co., 62 Mo. 313	161
Hart v. New Orleans, 12 Fed. Rep. 292	218
Harward v. St. Clair and Monroe Levee and Drainage Co., 51 Ill. 130	83
Hill v. Boston, 122 Mass. 344	109, 144, 151
Hill v. Charlotte, 72 N. C. 55	121
Hitchins v. Frostburg, 68 Md. 100	133
Holladay v. Frisbie, 15 Cal. 630	219
Hornbeck v. Westbrook, 9 Johnson, 73	101
Horton v. Mobile School Commissioners, 43 Alabama, 598	78
Howard v. Worcester, 153 Mass. 426	164
Indiana v. Worann, 6 Hill, N. Y. 33	180
In re. See name of case.	
Ireland v. Free Borough, 12 Coke, 120	243
Jackson v. Cory, 8 Johnson, 385	101
Jackson v. Hartwell, 8 Johnson, 422	101
Jackson v. Schoonmaker, 2 Johnson, 230	101
Johnston v. District of Columbia, 118 U. S. 19	129
Keble v. Philadelphia, 31 Pa. St. 41	153
Kelly v. Milwaukee, 127 U. S. 139	104
Kennedy v. New York, 73 N. Y. 365	152
Ketchum v. Buffalo, 14 N. Y. 356	50
Kiley v. City of Kansas, 87 Mo. 103	119
Kincaid v. Hardin, 53 Iowa, 430	154

	PAGE
Kings County Insurance Company *v.* Stevens, 101 N. Y. 411	212
Kinkle *v.* Franklin, 13 Minn. 127	105
Kline *v.* The Parish of Ascension, 33 La. Ann. 562	215
La Clef *v.* The City of Concordia, 41 Kans. 323	140
Lafayette *v.* Alick, 81 Ind. 166	175, 177
Langford *v.* United States, 101 U. S. 341	106, 112
Lansing *v.* Toolan, 37 Mich. 152	130
Laramie County *v.* Albany County, 92 U. S. 307	194
Layton *v.* New Orleans, 12 La. Ann. 515	28, 31
Lewis *v.* State, 96 N. Y. 71	107
Lloyd *v.* The Mayor, etc., of New York, 5 N. Y. 347	111
Loan Association *v.* Topeka, 20 Wallace, 655	102
Lord *v.* Oconto, 47 Wis. 386	212
Louisville *v.* Com., 1 Duval, Ky. 295	217
Lowe *v.* Board, 94 Ind. 553	216
Marks *v.* Pardue, 37 Ind. 155	103
Matter of, In the. See name of case.	
Matthews *v.* City of Alexandria, 68 Mo. 115	212
Mayor of Baltimore *v.* State, 15 Md. 576	208
Mayor, etc., of New York *v.* Tenth National Bank, 111 N. Y. 446	87
Maximilian *v.* The Mayor, etc., of New York, 62 N. Y. 160	139
McCarthy *v.* Commonwealth, 110 Pa. St. 243	72, 82
McCaughey *v.* Tritt, 12 R. I. 449	171
McCoull *v.* The City of Manchester, 85 Va. 579	126
McDade *v.* Chester City, 117 Pa. St. 414	119
McDonough's Executors *v.* Murdock, 15 How. U. S. 363	50
Mead *v.* New Haven, 40 Conn. 42	136
Mercer *v.* Pittsburgh Railroad Company, 36 Pa. St. 99	207
Meriwether *v.* Garrett, 102 U. S. 472	31, 214
Merrick *v.* Amherst, 12 Allen, Mass. 500	103
Metropolitan Board of Excise *v.* Barrie, 34 N. Y. 657	43

	PAGE
Metropolitan Board of Health v. Heister, 37 N. Y. 661	80, 89
Milam Co. v. Bateman, 54 Tex. 153	206
Milhau v. Sharp, 15 Barbour, N. Y. 193	147
Milwaukee, Town of, v. City of Milwaukee, 12 Wis. 93,	194
Moffitt v. The City of Asheville, 103 N. C. 237	140
Montpelier v. East Montpelier, 29 Vt. 12	188, 193
Morgan v. Beloit, 7 Wall. 613	194
Mortland v. Christian, 52 N. J. Law, 521	81
Moulton v. Scarborough, 71 Me. 267	158
Mount Hope Cemetery Co. v. Boston, 158 Mass. 509	197
Mulcairns v. The City of Janesville, 29 N. W. Rep. 565	174
Municipality No. 3 v. Hart, 6 La. Ann. 570	214, 218
Munn v. Illinois, 94 U. S. 113	38
Murphy v. Lowell, 124 Mass. 564	153
Nashville v. Ray, 19 Wallace, 468	51
Neuert v. The City of Boston, 120 Mass. 339	171
New Jersey v. Wilson, 7 Cranch, 164	40
New Orleans v. Clarke, 95 U. S. 644	31
New Orleans v. Morris, 105 U. S. 600	216
New Orleans v. Morris, 3 Woods, C. C. 103	220
New Orleans v. Home Mutual Ins. Co., 23 La. Ann. 61,	218
N. O. M. & T. R. R. Co. v. Ellerman, 105 U. S. 166	200
N. O. & C. R. R. Co. v. Municipality No. 1, 7 La. Ann. 148	215
North Hempstead v. Hempstead, 2 Wendell, N. Y. 109	101
Olcott v. Supervisors, 16 Wall. 678	105
Oliver v. Worcester, 102 Mass. 489	151
Ould v. Richmond, 23 Grattan, 464	17
Pawlet, Town of, v. Clark, 9 Cranch, 292	186, 188
Pennsylvania Hall, In re, 5 Pa. St. 204	28
People v. Albertson, 55 N. Y. 50	88
People v. Batchellor, 53 N. Y. 128	52, 104
People v. Chicago, 51 Ill. 17	84, 129
People v. Detroit, 28 Mich. 228	84, 199

	PAGE
People v. Draper, 15 N. Y. 532	21, 80, 89, 208
People v. Fields, 58 N. Y. 491	192
People v. Henshaw, 76 Cal. 436	85
People v. Hows, 37 Barb. 440	28
People v. Hurlbut, 24 Mich. 44	84
People v. Ingersoll, 58 N. Y. 1	191
People v. Kerr, 27 N. Y. 188	142, 207
People v. Lynch, 51 Cal. 15	86
People v. Mahaney, 13 Mich. 481	88
People v. Mayor, 15 Md. 376	88
People v. Pinckney, 32 N. Y. 397	80, 89
Perkins v. Slack, 86 Pa. St. 283	25, 52, 87
Pfefferle v. The Commissioners, 39 Kans. 432	140
Philadelphia v. Field, 58 Pa. St. 320	87
Philadelphia v. Fox, 64 Pa. St. 169	193
Plimpton v. Somerset, 33 Vt. 283	28
Police Jury of Plaquemines v. Foulhouze, 30 La. Ann. 64	215
Police Jury of West Baton Rouge v. Michel, 4 La. Ann. 84	214
Prather v. Lexington 13 B. Monroe Ky. 559	135
President, etc. v. Indianapolis, 12 Ind. 620	216
Pruther v. Lexington, 13 B. Monroe, 559	135
Pumphrey v. Baltimore, 47 Md. 145	87
Purdy v. The People, 4 Hill, N. Y. 384	58
Ransom v. Boal, 29 Iowa, 68	211
Rex v. London, 8 How. St. Tr. 1039, 1340	244
Rivers v. City Council of Augusta, 65 Ga. 376	120
Robinson v. The City of Evansville, 87 Ind. 334	138
Rogers v. Burlington, 3 Wallace, 654	31
Roper v. McWhorter, 77 Va. 214	203
Rowland v. Kalamazoo Co. Supts., 49 Mich. 553	159
Russell v. Men of Devon, 2 T. R. 672	100
Ryerson v. Utley, 16 Mich. 269	104
Sanborn v. Rice County, 9 Minn. 273	28
Sayre Borough v. Phillips, 148 Pa. St. 482	16
Schaffer v. Cadwallader, 36 Pa. St. 126	217

	PAGE
Schumacher v. Toberman, 56 Cal. 508	86
Seaman v. New York, 80 N. Y. 239	152
Seifert v. The City of Brooklyn, 101 N. Y. 136	132
Semmes v. Columbus, 19 Ga. 471	213
Shad v. Crawford, 3 Metc. Ky. 207	88
Shannon v. O'Boyle, 51 Ind. 565	213
Smith v. Barrett & Clifford, 1 Siderfin, 161	210
Sparkes v. Mayor, 21 Pa. St. 147	105
Spaulding v. Andover, 54 N. H. 38	204
Speir v. The City of Brooklyn, 139 N. Y. 6	124
Stackhouse v. Lafayette, 26 Ind. 17	129
Stanley v. City of Davenport, 54 Iowa, 463	125
State v. B. and O. R. R. Co., 12 Gill & Johnson, Md. 399	31
State v. B. and O. R. R. Co., 3 Howard, U. S. 534	31
State v. Baughman, 39 Ohio St. 455	80
State v. Clinton, 26 La. Ann. 561	103
State v. County Court of Jackson County, 89 Mo. 237	71, 86
State v. County Court of St. Louis, 34 Mo. 546	208
State v. Covington, 29 Ohio St. 111	80, 90
State v. Denny, 118 Ind. 382	88
State v. Hammer, 42 N. J. Law, 485	66
State v. Haven, 22 Wis. 660	205
State v. Herrmann, 75 Mo. 340	71
State v. Hunter, 38 Kans. 578	88
State v. Mayor, 20 Atlantic Reporter, 886	77
State v. Newark, 40 N. J. Law, 550	58
State v. Philbrick, 15 Atlantic Reporter, 579	76, 86
State v. Pugh, 43 Ohio St. 98	70, 81
State v. Schweickardt, 19 S. W. Rep. 47	199
State v. Seavey, 22 Neb. 474	88
State v. Simon, 22 Atlantic Reporter, 120	74, 82
State v. Smith, 44 Ohio St. 348	85
State v. Tappan, 29 Wis. 664	28, 104
State v. Tiedman, 69 Mo. 306	215

State v. Township Committee of Northampton, 14 Atlantic Reporter, 587	72, 79
State v. Warner, 4 Washington, 773	81
State v. Woodward, 23 Vt. 92	212
Stetson v. Kempton, 13 Mass. 272	104
Stewart v. The Supervisors, 83 Ill. 341	140
Still v. Lansingburgh, 16 Barbour, N. Y. 107	211
Suffolk v. Parker, 79 Va. 660	153
Supervisors of Warren Co. v. Patterson, 56 Ill. 111	212
Taintor v. Worcester, 123 Mass. 311	138
Terre Haute v. Terre Haute Water Works Co., 70 Ind. 305	213
Terrett v. Taylor, 9 Cranch, 43	186
Thomas v. Leland, 24 Wendell, N. Y. 65	103
Thomson v. Ashworth, 73 Cal. 73	85
Tindley v. The City of Salem, 137 Mass. 171	157
Toledo v. Cone, 41 Ohio St. 149	152
Topeka v. Gillette, 32 Kans. 431	72
Traphagen v. Jersey City, 29 N. J. Eq. 206	147
United States v. Baltimore and Ohio R. R. Co., 17 Wallace, 322	31
United States v. De Groot, 5 Wall. 419	106
United States v. Eckford, 6 Wall. 434	106
United States v. McDaniel, 7 Peters, 16	106
Van Pelt v. Davenport, 42 Iowa, 208	131
Van Riper v. Parsons, 40 N. J. Law, 123	67
Vasser v. George, 47 Miss. 713	28
Ward v. County of Hartford, 12 Conn. 406	100
Webb v. The Mayor of New York, 64 Howard's Pr. 10	203
West Co. of Howe v. Cleveland, 12 Ohio St. 589	135
Western Savings Society v. Philadelphia, 31 Pa. St. 175	153
Westport, City of, v. Kansas City, 103 Mo. 141	81
Wheeler v. Philadelphia, 77 Pa. St. 338	69, 92
White v. Yazoo City, 37 Miss. 357	136
Whiting v. Sheboygan R'y Co., 25 Wis. 167	105

	PAGE
Wilcox v. Chicago, 107 Ill. 334	114, 138
Wild v. Paterson, 47 N. J. Law, 40	177
Williamsport v. Com., 84 Pa. St. 487	51
Wilson v. Board of Trustees, 27 N. E. Rep. 203	80
Wixon v. Newport, 13 R. I. 454	164
Wyandotte, City of, v. Wood, 5 Kans. 603	81

ADDENDA ET CORRIGENDA.

P. 56. Idaho (III. 19) and Kansas (XII. 1) forbid special incorporation acts.

P. 60. Colorado (X. 7), Idaho (VII. 6), Missouri (X. 10), Montana (XII. 4), and Nebraska (IX. 6 and 7) should be added to list of states prohibiting the imposition of taxes for corporate purposes. Reference to Illinois constitution should read IX. 10.

P. 61, note 3, Georgia (III. 7, p. 20) should be added to the list.

TABLE OF CONTENTS

CHAPTER I

	PAGE
INTRODUCTION	1
American and European municipal government	1
Original American municipal organization	2
Disintegration of municipal council	3
Popular election of municipal officers	4
Growth of the powers of the mayor	5
European municipal organization	6
Difficulties in the way of good municipal government	7

CHAPTER II

THE PUBLIC CHARACTER OF AMERICAN MUNICIPAL CORPORATIONS, AND THE FAILURE OF THE LEGISLATURE TO SET ASIDE A SPHERE OF MUNICIPAL HOME RULE	11
Origin of municipal corporations in England	12
Private character of English municipal government	13
Degeneration of English municipal government	14
Original character of American municipal government	15
Growth of the public side of American cities	17
Double character of municipal corporations	18
Failure of legislature to recognize their private side	19
Relation of New York to the legislature	20
Extent of legislative regulation of municipal affairs	22
Philadelphia City Hall	25

	PAGE
Legislative interference often due to partisan politics	26
Payment of claims against cities	27
Present position of cities in New York State	28
Legislature not subject to control of courts	30

CHAPTER III

THE EFFECT OF THE AMERICAN SYSTEM OF PROTECTING PRIVATE RIGHTS UPON THE ATTITUDE OF THE LEGISLATURE TOWARDS MUNICIPAL CORPORATIONS . 33

Protection of private rights by the constitution as interpreted by the courts	34
Disadvantages of the method	36
Apt to confuse public privilege with private right	37
Bad effect of such confusion on the position of municipal corporations	40
Relieves legislature of sense of responsibility	41

CHAPTER IV

THE EFFECTS OF THE AMERICAN LAW AS TO MUNICIPAL POWERS ON THE ATTITUDE OF THE LEGISLATURE TOWARDS MUNICIPAL CORPORATIONS . 45

Narrow municipal powers	46
Necessary application to legislature for power	47
Narrow financial powers	49
Constitutional limitation of borrowing powers	52
Encroachment of legislature natural	54

CHAPTER V

THE CONSTITUTIONAL LIMITATIONS OF THE POWER OF THE LEGISLATURE OVER MUNICIPAL AFFAIRS . . 56

General incorporation acts made obligatory	57
Special acts relative to certain municipal affairs forbidden	59

	PAGE
Local elections provided	60
Acts general in form may be special	63
Classification of cities permitted	65
Class may consist of one city when made	66
Population proper basis of classification	68
Classification made for present not proper	71
Geographical classification not proper	74
"Municipal affairs" not clearly defined	78
"Municipal affairs" embrace matters of general importance	79
Boundaries and duties and salaries of officers not to be regulated by special act	81
What are "corporate powers"	83
Constitutional right of cities to local self-government	84
Local assessments and taxation by special act improper	86
What is a municipal officer	87
Police officers	88
Classification of cities by constitution	92
Dangers of such a method	93
Narrow meaning of "special act"	95
Prohibition of special legislation not successful	96
New constitution of New York	97

CHAPTER VI

The Means of Delimiting the Sphere of Private Action of Municipal Corporations in the American Law	99
English idea of local self-government	99
Decentralization of the system in the United States	100
Introduction of idea of local corporations	101
Constitutional protection of local corporate property	102
Local taxation for local purposes	103
Local corporations liable on contracts	106

	PAGE
When liable for tort	107
Private local property alienable	108
Corporate idea a continental idea	109

CHAPTER VII

WHAT ARE MUNICIPAL AFFAIRS FROM THE POINT OF VIEW OF THE LIABILITY OF MUNICIPAL CORPORATIONS FOR TORTS 111

Double character of municipal corporations	111
Government not responsible for torts	112
Government acts as a private individual	114
When it so acts, is responsible for torts by German and French law	116
Municipal corporations not responsible for torts when acting as government	118
Is so acting when exercising legislative powers	119
Also when exercising discretionary powers	127
Except when it adopts a manifestly defective plan for public works	131
Acts as government when exercising police powers	133
Police powers used in broad sense	136
Acts as government in the care of the poor	139
Is responsible for tort in managing institutions for purely local benefit	141
Municipal corporations have no property in streets, but are liable for not maintaining them	142
Quasi-corporations not responsible	144
Reason for liability in case of streets	146
Quasi-corporations by statute liable for highways	148
Duty to care for property, basis for liability for tort	149

CHAPTER VIII

WHAT ARE MUNICIPAL AFFAIRS FROM THE POINT OF VIEW OF THE LIABILITY OF MUNICIPAL CORPORATIONS FOR THEIR MANAGEMENT OF PROPERTY . . 150

Application of rule of liability for tort to property . . 150
Agreement as to liability for revenue-bearing property . 151
Conflict in the recent decisions as to public property . 153
Quasi-corporations not liable for public property . . 154
Qualification of exemption in Bigelow *v.* Randolph . . 155
Quasi-corporations liable for revenue-bearing property . 157
Unwarranted extension of rule in Bigelow *v.* Randolph 160
Ground of exemption of *quasi*-corporations found in the generally public character of their duties 163
Same rule applied to municipal corporations in early decisions 164
This rule abandoned in recent decisions 166
Reasons given unsatisfactory 168
Duty to maintain property in good condition private . 174
Advantages of this view 179
Public policy does not require exemption from liability . 180

CHAPTER IX

WHAT MUNICIPAL PROPERTY IS PROTECTED BY THE CONSTITUTIONAL PROVISIONS PROTECTING PRIVATE PROPERTY 184

Reluctance of courts to accord protection 185
Property held by municipal corporations in trust protected 186
But the trustee may be changed 193
Property used for local purposes protected 194
Land is such local property 196
So also a cemetery 197
So also parks 198

	PAGE
And ferries and wharves	200
And water works	203
Property used for governmental purposes, such as streets, not protected	207
And property used for police purposes	208

CHAPTER X

What municipal property is subject to alienation

	209
Private municipal property alienable	210
But not public property, such as a common	211
Nor a park	212
Private municipal property may be sold on execution	213
Claims for taxes are not such private property	214
Nor public buildings used for governmental purposes	215
Nor water works	216
Income-bearing property generally subject to execution	218
Contradictory views of courts explained	220

CHAPTER XI

What is the sphere of private municipal action recognized by the American law

	221
Boundaries of cities not to be changed by special act	222
Nor general organization	223
Nor official salaries and duties	224
Police powers not local	224
Public works generally local	225
Property held for revenue local	226
Liability for torts in connection with property	228
What is sphere of local action	229
This is not always protected from legislative encroachment	230

CHAPTER XII

	PAGE
European methods of distinguishing and securing the sphere of municipal home rule	233
Original system of English local government	234
Poor-law amendment act of 1834	235
Formation of special local authorities for general functions of government	236
Subject to a central administrative control	237
Public health and education	238
Public charity and police	239
Grants of large local powers to local corporations	241
Municipal government prior to 1835	242
Cities sacrificed to national politics	243
Crusade against municipal corporations	244
Municipal corporations act of 1835	245
Recent development of English cities	246
New system of administrative control	247
Does away with necessity of special legislation	249
How sphere of municipal government has been distinguished on the continent	251
Conception of local corporations	252
General grant of local powers	253
General municipal corporations acts	254
Central administrative control	255
Makes special legislation unnecessary	256
Cities discharge functions of general government	257
Characteristics of American administrative system	259
Absence of administrative control	260
Destruction of legislative control by constitution	261
Attitude of courts towards constitution	262
Its explanation	264
Its good results	265
Original American system of local administration no longer useful	266

	PAGE
Changes in it proposed	267
Recent development of administrative control in United States	268
Over local corporations	269
When legislature has been deprived of powers of special legislation	270
Probable further development of the central administrative control over cities	271
INDEX	273

MUNICIPAL HOME RULE

CHAPTER I

INTRODUCTION

PERHAPS no part of the American system of government has caused such dissatisfaction as the government of our cities. This dissatisfaction has been due undoubtedly in part to the imperfect performance of numerous and important duties, which, in a new country like the United States, our cities have been obliged to assume, and which they could hardly have been expected to perform much better than they have performed them. The work of American cities has been greater perhaps than that of European cities, not only on account of the newness of the country, which made it necessary to do what had to be done at once,[1] but also because of the characteristic willingness and even eagerness of the American people to make imme-

---

[1] Cf. the remarks of Hon. Seth Low in the chapter on Municipal Government in Bryce's *American Commonwealth*, Vol. I., p. 620.

diate use of any invention which will increase their comfort or save their time. The very general use of the streets in cities for the distribution of water, heat, gas, and electricity in its manifold forms has vastly increased the burdens which have been imposed upon the American city.

But with all due allowance made for the greater tasks which American municipal government has been called upon to perform,[1] the fact undoubtedly is, that as compared with the larger and best governed European cities, the larger and best governed American cities have been in the past, and are, although to a less degree, in the present, unwisely, inefficiently, and extravagantly administered. When the dissatisfaction with municipal conditions first became apparent, the remedy which it was at first sought to apply was change in organization.

The municipal organization which first obtained in this country was, like most of our governmental institutions, an importation from England rather than an indigenous growth. It consisted in a municipal council in which, or in whose members, were concentrated almost all functions of munici-

---

[1] Too much stress should not be laid upon this point, for all large cities, as well in Europe as in this country, are comparatively recent developments. See Shaw, *Municipal Government in Great Britain*, pp. 5, 6.

pal government. The change in this organization which was at first proposed and adopted was the incorporation into it of the checks and balances which characterized the national government, and whose efficacy in promoting and assuring good government it was, at the time, deemed political heresy to doubt. The mayor, who had been a member of the council, became very generally independent thereof. The judicial functions of the members of the council were very generally assigned in the larger cities to special municipal judges no longer members of the council. Finally the council was, after national models, very generally organized as a bicameral body.

This change did not, however, work all the good that was expected of it, and in their impatience at seeing their property still wasted, and their cities still poorly administered, the people applied a second time to municipal misgovernment what seemed to them an unfailing and infallible panacea. This time it was democracy. The period from 1830 to 1850 was marked the world over by the growth of an overweening confidence in the wisdom, the greatness, and the goodness of the people. All evils in government were to be done away with by bringing the people as near as might be to the seats of governmental power. In the United States, in the country at large as well as in the cities, this belief resulted in a widening of the suffrage until it became universal manhood suffrage, and in the grant to the people of the power to elect almost all officers of government. In the cities particularly, the important change in organization which resulted was the election by universal manhood suffrage, not only of the mayor and council, but also of the heads of the various executive departments which had originally been under the control of committees of the council, as they are still in England, but which, after the first reform of American municipal institutions, had sprung into an independent existence.

Again were the people doomed to disappointment, and, if we may judge of municipal conditions by contemporary criticism and literature, their last state was worse than their first. The extremely loose and disconnected organization adopted by the democratic movement of the first half of the century made necessary the formation of "Rings" and "Deals" if municipal government was to go on at all. What made matters worse was the profound disappointment and distrust of reform and change, the loss of confidence in the worth or wisdom of the people, which was extremely unsettling in a naturally democratic community. This lost, no one knew which way to turn. But something had to be done, and with that practical common sense which has ever been the saving of this community, although it has always prided itself on its consistent adherence to certain political theories, it was determined to turn the back on all the allurements and temptations of democracy, and infuse into our municipal government more of that monarchical principle which it had been the custom to deride, but a *modicum* of which is necessary to the existence of all government. This was effected by increasing very largely the powers of the mayor, who has been placed at the head of the municipal government with a plenitude of power which is unexampled in the aristocratic society and monarchical governments of Europe. In all the larger cities the later charters give the mayor almost absolute power of appointing most of the important heads of departments, and in many cases add thereto the power of removal; and the tendency seems everywhere to magnify the importance of his position.

This is the stage of municipal development in which we find ourselves at present, and it is regarded by most municipal reformers as quite unorthodox to doubt the final efficacy for good government of this particular form of municipal organization. Yet at the same time, it may not be amiss to point out that in England and also, though not to the same extent, on the continent, whose cities are set before us as shining examples of what our cities are not, *i.e.* well governed communities, the old form of municipal organization in accordance with which all powers are concentrated in a council still prevails, has indeed steadily prevailed during the period in which we have been pursuing the will-o'-the-wisp of good city government, through paths which have led us pretty close to the point from which we started. It may well be susceptible of doubt, therefore, whether any of the paths which we have so far trod is the one which we can safely hope will lead us to the desired goal; whether our failure has been due, to so great a degree as has been imagined, to a faulty municipal organization, or, at any rate, to a faulty theory of the distribution of powers among the various important municipal organs. One fault in municipal organization, and one to which until of recent years little attention has been directed, has unquestionably been a serious one. That is one which has characterized not only our municipal but indeed our entire governmental organization. It is the spoils system, and is only now being remedied in our national government. In course of time it may be corrected as well in our municipal organization, and until that is accomplished little hope of improvement can be entertained from any mere change in organization.

Apart from this, however, which is, of course, a serious fault, it is difficult, in the light of European experience, to comprehend why, other conditions being equal, we might not have enjoyed as good government in our cities as it seems to be admitted exists in Europe, under any one of the various forms of municipal organization to which we have resorted within the century that is now closing. But, as a matter of fact, conditions have not been the same in this country as in Europe. In the first place, social conditions have been and are very dissimilar. In America, owing to the habits of the people, the population is fluctuating, and as a result attachment to place is not strong. The universal race for wealth in which all who would win must pursue their course with untiring devotion and inflexible application, and which has been more attractive in our cities than elsewhere owing to the greater value of the prizes possible of attainment, has caused the more intelligent, if not the better classes of the communities, to look down upon, or at least to look with indifference upon, civic honours. These have on that account not only become accessible to, but have, except in times of great stress, when municipal patriotism has been more than usually aroused, actually been monopolized by persons of inferior intelligence and character, incapable of rendering to the community service of the highest value.

These are conditions which show little tendency to change, conditions which will always tend to increase the difficulty of obtaining permanent good city government in this country. We cannot expect that any change in our laws and institutions will cause them to disappear. But, in addition to them, there are other conditions, legal rather than social, in which American municipal life differs profoundly from that of Europe, and which have aggravated the evil influence of those already referred to. These are, indeed, almost sufficient to account for that lack of civic patriotism shown by even well-intentioned municipal citizens, and without which as a basis, no city can be well governed. They are the small sphere of local autonomy assigned by our law to our cities, and the continual interference in city affairs of the central commonwealth legislature. This interference has been due very largely to the despair of the people in our cities of ever obtaining good government through their own efforts. They have, therefore, rushed to the legislature for protection. It has also been in some, if not in great measure, due to the prostitution of the cities in the interest of national and state politics with which municipal politics have always been and are now closely connected. We have repeated in America the experience of England before the Municipal Corporations Act of 1835. What we need to arouse local interest is the application of the same remedy which has been applied in England, *i.e.* the grant to municipalities of such a degree of local autonomy or home rule as will cause all municipal citizens to feel a healthy sense of responsibility for the evils from which they suffer, as well as an assured conviction that they have it in their power to work a sensible improvement in their condition.

The ideal way in which to accomplish this result would of course be for the legislature to abdicate its power to interfere in local matters and to distinguish a sphere of action on the part of municipalities into which it should not intrude. But the legislature has had it in its power from the beginning to pursue this course, which it has distinctly refused to take. It is idle, therefore, to hope that it will at this hour of the day alter its conduct. The only way left, it was thought, was by tying the hands of the legislature by the constitution, to prevent it from interfering in strictly municipal affairs. But just as soon as this is done we find ourselves in a position of great difficulty. For it is a dangerous thing to tie the hands of the law-making power. We cannot see far enough in the future to know whether in all instances the knot will have been wisely tied. We cannot, without considerable study, determine how tightly that knot should be tied, and what it should embrace. American cities do so much work which is not municipal in the sense of having only a local interest, that, admitting the wisdom or necessity in present American conditions of forbidding the legislature to interfere in local affairs, it becomes necessary to determine what are local affairs.

It is the purpose of this little work to inquire how successful this method of municipal reform has been, and to determine, from a consideration of the various branches of the law of municipal corporations which will throw any light on the subject, what is the sphere of action in which a city moves as a local authority, — what, if any, is the sphere of municipal home rule in which it should be allowed to move free from central control. It is believed that the delimitation of such a sphere is important, for all concrete attempts at municipal reform through both this constitutionalizing of the city's position as well as through the methods adopted in Europe to accomplish the same ultimate end, are dependent upon the conclusions arrived at with regard to it.

Occasion will be taken to touch in passing also upon European municipal conditions, in order to ascertain if we may hope to learn anything from the experience of those who have had the same problems as we have had to solve, and who, it seems to be generally admitted, have been more successful than we have been in their solution.

CHAPTER II

THE PUBLIC CHARACTER OF AMERICAN MUNICIPAL CORPORATIONS, AND THE FAILURE OF THE LEGISLATURE TO SET ASIDE A SPHERE OF MUNICIPAL HOME RULE

THE origin of municipal corporations is everywhere the same. It is to be found in the grant to certain sections of the country in which were to be found comparatively large aggregations of people, of a series of privileges. Originally throughout the Teutonic world, there were no municipal corporations. Indeed, there was no municipal government from the legal point of view. In early Germany, the only actual cities that existed were of Roman origin, and generally with the overthrow of Rome, what had been municipalities, became, legally, simply parts of the county or duchy in which they were situated. The inhabitants of such sections were, until the grant to them of special privileges, like the inhabitants of the outlying and rural districts, subject to the governmental power of the duke or count. But soon the peculiar social and economic conditions of the thickly populated districts began to differ from those of the rural districts, and this difference in social and economic conditions brought with it a change in the law by which cities were to be governed. The rights which were obtained finally by cities, were in England, to which our attention will be directed, in the words of Bishop Stubbs:[1] "Free election of magistrates, independent exercise of jurisdiction in their own courts, and by their own customs, and the direct negotiation of their taxation with the officers of the Exchequer." These, as Bishop Stubbs remarks, were no unimportant steps in the attainment of municipal independence at a time when most officers of the government were appointed by the Crown, and when the country, as a whole, was governed by certain general rules of popular law, and was subject to be taxed through the sheriffs, who were always most unpopular officers. While in their origin, municipal boroughs were distinguished from the rural districts by their possession of privileges, which were of a public legal rather than a private legal character, soon as a result of the grant to them of charters of incorporation, they began to assume considerably more of a private character. The first charter of incorporation appears to have

[1] *Constitutional History of England*, Vol. I., p. 628.

been granted to the city of Kingston-upon-Hull, in 1429,[1] but the incorporation of municipal boroughs does not assume such proportions as to be capable of being styled a movement until the accession of the Tudors to the throne of England. The purpose of these charters of incorporation was to make the boroughs, after the example of the canon law, artificial subjects of private law, so as to permit them more easily to own property and to sue and be sued. Their effect was merely to emphasize the private side of municipal life, and they had little or no immediate and direct influence upon the governmental position of the boroughs. The corporation formed by such a charter consisted not of the whole community, but of certain persons, as a matter of fact the most important persons in the community. As a result of the peculiar political conditions which afterwards obtained in England, these persons, who controlled the government of the borough, became subservient at first to the Crown, and later, that is, after the revolution of 1640 to 1688, to the nobles who then assumed the political power in the kingdom. The municipal boroughs were used as tools in the interest of national politics, and thus became almost incapacitated for the performance of any efficient administrative work. The

[1] Cox, *Institutions of the English Government*, p. 728.

later functions which the government began to assume subsequent to and partially as a result of the Reformation, were therefore put into the hands, not of the municipal corporation or its agents, but of officers who were to act in the limits of the municipal borough, as they acted in the rural districts, as mere agents of the central government. The municipal organization was so bad, as a result of the prostitution of municipal institutions in the interest of the national politics of the country, that not only were the various functions of central government, such as the care of the poor, the sanitary administration, and the administration of the public schools when they developed,[1] put into the hands of officers of the central government, but also the various new functions of municipal administration, the adoption of which was necessitated by the increase of population in the cities, were put into the hands, not of the municipal authorities, but of new authorities which were established by special and local legislation. Thus when it became necessary to provide for some method of lighting and paving the streets, these matters were entrusted, either to

[1] The care of the public health and of schools, both of which became only in this century the objects of governmental activity, was put into the hands of central authorities more as a result of tradition than because of the incapacity of the municipal administration, which had meanwhile been reformed by the act of 1835.

the parishes which had become organized under the legislation of the Tudors, or to special trusts or commissions which were formed for their care. This was done notwithstanding the fact that the inhabitants were forced to contribute by means of special rates to the expenses of those branches of administration.[1]

Such was the conception in England during the last century of the sphere of municipal activity. It will be noticed that this sphere was a very narrow one. It did not embrace even all the functions of local government; it embraced hardly any functions at all whose discharge interested the state as a whole. It was only natural that upon the formation of municipalities in this country the English conception of the sphere of activity attributed to them should have had great influence. Like the English municipal corporation, the original American municipal corporation was mainly an organization for the satisfaction of purely local needs, that is, for the management of local property and finances. It had, however, like the English municipal corporation, the power to issue local police ordinances, while certain of the officers of the corporation discharged a series of judicial and police functions. Thus, as was often the case in

---

[1] Gneist, *Self-government*, etc., 595. Blunden, "British Local Finance," *Political Science Quarterly*, Vol. IX., pp. 85, 86.

England, in both New York and Philadelphia, the mayor, recorder, and aldermen were, by the charter, made the municipal justices of the peace and judges.[1]

One of the results of the almost purely local and *quasi*-private character of the original American municipality was that the city council had no power to levy taxes in order to provide for the expenses of the local services. It was not regarded as a sufficiently governmental authority to be endowed with this attribute of sovereignty.[2]

Almost the only real governmental function possessed by early English and American municipal corporations as such, was the issue of local police ordinances, which, it is still held, municipal corporations have the right to issue, as a result of the fact of their being incorporated.[3]

While the original position of the American municipality has had great influence and is now of importance on the common law applicable to municipal corporations, still, as a result of various

---

[1] For New York, see the Charter of 1730, Secs. 23, 26, 27, and 31. For Philadelphia, see Johns Hopkins University Studies in History and Political Science, Vol. V., pp. 19 and 29.

[2] Black, "Municipal Ownership of Land on Manhattan Island; in *Studies in History, Economics, and Public Law*, edited by the University Faculty of Political Science of Columbia College, Vol. I., p. 182; also Johns Hopkins University Studies, etc., Vol. V., 27.

[3] Sayre Borough v. Phillips, 148 Pa. St. 482; 33 Amer. St. Rep. 842.

statutes which have been passed relative to municipal corporations, the actual position of the municipality and the duties to be attended to by its officers at the present time have greatly changed. The state legislature, which has the power to determine what shall be the functions of municipal corporations, has, to a large extent, lost sight of their original purpose, and has come to regard them as organs of the central government, for the purposes of the general state administration, and has thus made them more public in character than they originally were.

Thus, while by the common law even at present, the better rule would seem to be that the incorporation of a place does not carry with it the power to levy taxes,[1] as a result of statute almost all of the municipal corporations have, at the present time, the power to levy certain taxes.[2]

Further, in many cases the legislature has conferred powers of central government upon officers who are elected by the people of the cities, or appointed by the municipal authorities. Thus, for example, in most of the cities of the United States, municipal officers are entrusted with the

[1] Cooley, *Taxation*, 2d ed., p. 275, and cases cited.

[2] Dillon, *Law of Municipal Corporations*, 4th ed., Vol. I., p. 69. See, for an example of the general grant of the tax power sometimes made to cities, the case of Ould *v.* Richmond, 23 Grattan, Va., 464; 14 American Reports, 139.

preservation of the peace, the care of the public health, and the maintenance and management of jails and court buildings, attend to election matters, and often have a series of duties to perform relative to the administration of judicial affairs, such as the making up of jury lists. In some cases, also, the care of the poor and of the schools is devolved upon the cities. Finally, the corporation itself is sometimes made the direct agent of the central government, as, for example, in the collection of the state taxes.

As a matter of fact, therefore, most of the larger cities in the United States are at the present time not only organizations for the satisfaction of local needs, but also agents of the central government of the state, and are entrusted with the exercise of powers affecting not only the inhabitants of the local districts of which they have jurisdiction, but also the inhabitants of the whole state.

This double character of municipal corporations must of necessity have an important influence on their relation to the legislature, the only guardian in the American system of administration of administrative harmony and uniformity. For so long as a municipal corporation is merely an organization for local government, the legislature is not necessarily called upon to interfere with or control its actions except in so far as it is to lay down the general norms of its conduct, as in the case of all individuals subject to the obedience of the state. But just so soon as a municipal corporation begins to act as the agent of the state, to exercise powers of concern to the people of the state as a whole, it becomes necessary for the guardian of the people as a whole to see to it that these powers are exercised uniformly and efficiently throughout the state. Unfortunately, however, for American municipal corporations, the American legislature has not distinguished so clearly as it should have done, the two kinds of municipal activity, has in many cases forgotten that municipalities have a sphere of local action in which they should move freely and largely uncontrolled, and has perceived merely that, whatever may have been their original purpose and indeed should be their primary purpose at present, they are now state agents which are subject to its continual control, a control which it has not scrupled to exercise over all their actions, local as well as general. It has extended the control which the central government of the state should have and must frequently exercise over all matters attended to by the cities or their officers in which the people of the state as a whole are interested, over matters as well, in which the people of the state as a whole are not so interested, but which are of merely local and municipal interest.

The history of the relation of the city of New York to the legislature of the state of New York is an instructive example of this improper extension of legislative control. The city of New York received from the English kings during the colonial period a charter which, on the Declaration of the Independence of the colony of New York, and the establishment of the new state of New York, was confirmed by the first Constitution of the State.[1] For a considerable period after the adoption of this constitution, changes in that charter were made upon the initiation of the people of the city, which initiation took place through the medium of charter conventions whose members were elected by the people of the city, and no statute which was passed by the legislature of the state relative to the affairs of the city of New York took effect within the city until it had been approved by the city. About the middle of this century, the legislature was called upon to interfere in the administration by the city of certain matters which affected the state as a whole. One of the most marked examples of this central interference, made without the consent or approval of the city or its people, is to be found in the adoption of the metro-

[1] Article XXXVI.

politan police bill in 1857. The administration of the police in the period immediately preceding 1857 had been accompanied by great scandal and was regarded as extremely inefficient. Partly because of this, and partly, it is believed, for reasons of partisan politics, the legislature provided for the formation of a metropolitan police district, which embraced all of the territory of New York city, and also the territory of certain outlying districts, and placed at the head of this district a police commission appointed by the Governor and Senate. On account of the unprecedented character of such an act, the people of New York, led by the mayor, attempted to resist the enforcement of the bill; and such resistance led to positive bloodshed. The question, however, was finally referred to the courts, and the Court of Appeals[1] held that the action of the legislature was perfectly proper, inasmuch as the administration of the police was not a local function, but was a matter which affected the state as a whole, and might therefore be put into the hands of authorities having jurisdiction over a territory greater than that of any one city, and appointed by the central government of the state.

The success of the legislature in thus interfering in what had been considered by the people of New

[1] People v. Draper, 15 N. Y., 532.

York a branch of municipal administration, led it to carry its interference into other branches where its action could not be so well justified. In addition to centralizing in the same way the administration of the fire department and the administration of the public health and of excise legislation, *i.e.* liquor legislation, the legislature provided for a commission to attend to the public parks, which were evidently a matter of purely local concern. It has within recent years appointed an aqueduct and a rapid transit commission, both bodies attending not to state, but to municipal business. The application of the principle thus established, has been of great disadvantage to the government of the various cities within the state, and, as has been pointed out by the Hon. Seth Low,[1] "the habit of interference in city action has become to the legislature almost a second nature."

The legislature often claims to decide what salaries the cities shall pay its officers. The same authority says, that, "in every year of his term of office [as mayor of Brooklyn] he was compelled to oppose at Albany, legislation seeking to make an increase in the pay of policemen and firemen without any reference to the financial ability of the

---

[1] In his chapter on Municipal Government, contained in Bryce's *American Commonwealth*, first American edition, Vol. I., p. 630.

city, or the other demands upon the city for the expenditure of money." [1]

The legislature has often claimed also the right to appoint municipal officers and to fix and change the details of municipal organization, has legislated municipal officers out of office, and established new offices. In certain cases it has even provided that certain specific city streets shall be paved, has imposed burdens upon cities for the purpose of constructing sewers or bringing in water; has regulated the methods of transportation to be adopted within the limits of cities; in a word, has attended to a great number of matters which are purely local in character; matters which do not affect the people of the state as a whole, and in regard to which there is little excuse for special legislative action.

The extent to which this legislative regulation of local affairs has been carried, may be seen from the statements made in the report of the Fassett Committee of the New York Senate, appointed in 1890, to investigate the subject of municipal government in the state of New York. This shows that within six years (1884–1889, inclusive) the legislature of New York passed 1284 acts relative to the thirty cities in the state. Of these, 390 acts affected the city of New York.[2] In one year,

[1] *Ibid.*   [2] *Senate Committee Report,* Vol. V., p. 459.

viz., 1886, 280 of the 681 acts passed by the legislature, *i.e.* between one-third and one-half of its entire work, interfered directly with the affairs of some particular county, city, village, or town, specifically and expressly named.

The continual exercise of the powers of the legislature, relative to municipal affairs, has resulted in the gradual assumption by the legislature, in many parts of this country, of a long series of purely local powers. It has not limited its powers of control over municipalities to those matters in which such bodies were acting as agents of the central government, but has come to regard itself as a proper organ for local as well as central government. This centralization of local functions has had a most disastrous effect upon the cities of the United States; causing not only a great lack of local interest in the management of local affairs, but also an ignorant and inefficient management of these affairs — an unwise solution of many of the problems which have been presented to our cities. This result would seem to be almost unavoidable where local powers are exercised by a central body which of necessity can be but very slightly acquainted with local conditions, and which lacks all local responsibility. For the legislature, not being really representative of the various municipalities, cannot, in the nature of things, have that sense of responsibility to the municipalities which officers elected by their local constituents must feel. The Philadelphia City Hall Building affords a good example of how far this lack of local responsibility may sometimes carry the legislature in the exercise of local powers, and in the imposition of financial burdens on cities. "In 1870 the legislature decided that the city should have new buildings. The act [which was passed to accomplish this result] selected certain citizens by name, whom it appointed commissioners for the erection of the buildings. It made this body perpetual by authorizing it to fill vacancies. . . . This commission was imposed by the legislature upon the city, and given absolute control to create debts for the purpose named, and to require the levy of taxes for their payment."[1]

"The public buildings at Broad and Market Streets were," in the words of Judge Paxson,[2] "projected upon a scale of magnificence better suited for the capital of an empire than the municipal buildings of a debt-burdened city." Yet this act was declared constitutional, the city was compelled to supply the necessary funds,[3] and "for nearly twenty years all the money that could be spared from immediate and pressing

[1] Dillon, *Municipal Corporations*, 4th ed., Vol. I., p. 128.
[2] Perkins v. Slack, 86 Pa. St. 283.   [3] *Ibid.* p. 270.

needs" was "compulsorily expended upon an enormous pile which surpasses the town halls and cathedrals of the Middle Ages in extent if not in grandeur."[1] The control of the legislature over the finances of municipal corporations has, on account of its entire lack of local responsibility, been of so little value in preventing their extravagance, which is, of course, one of its most important *raisons d'être*, indeed it has so frequently been made use of to force them into undertakings involving great financial burdens, that it has been of late greatly limited by constitutional provision.[2]

The evil effects of legislative regulation of municipal affairs have been further aggravated by the fact that this central interference has in many instances been caused not by the desire on the part of the legislature to reform municipal abuses or to grant powers whose exercise is desired by the cities, but by the hope of deriving some temporary political advantage for the party in control of the central government of the state. It has not infrequently happened that changes in municipal organization have been made with the purpose of granting to some municipal officers in harmony in political feeling with the party in a majority in the central state government, large powers of appoint-

---

[1] Hare, *American Constitutional Law*, Vol. I., p. 630.
[2] See *infra*, p. 52.

ment. The city has been too often a pawn in the game of central politics to be sacrificed in the interest of some presumed partisan political advantage.

Special acts have been passed also to force the payment of claims not capable of enforcement in the courts, but held by persons possessed of political influence. The remarks of Mr. Justice O'Brien [1] are indicative of the extent to which this practice has been carried. He says: "It will be difficult to cite a more flagrant instance than the one here existing of a legislative act attempting to fasten on property owners a burden which the courts and local authorities have stamped as fraudulent and void. After defeat in the courts, the legislature was successfully applied to and a mandatory act passed which compelled the local authorities to assess, as part of the cost, work done under a contract which was fraudulent in its inception, was never complied with, and was finally abandoned." "Such action," says Judge Cooley,[2] "as against a natural person, would be clearly judicial, and therefore beyond legislative competency; and it could only be sustained in the case of municipal corporations on the doctrine that their powers and rights are wholly at the legislative disposal;

---

[1] In the Matter of Cullen, 53 Hun, 534.
[2] *Taxation*, 2d ed., p. 687.

a doctrine dangerous in government, and, as we think, unsound in constitutional law. The opinion has sometimes been expressed that these corporations were entitled to the constitutional benefits of an ordinary trial.[1] But this is denied in other cases, and perhaps a hearing before some court or board of audit might be all that a corporation could demand.[2] But such a hearing, if local municipal government is a matter of substance, they must be entitled to."

The condition of things which this centralization of local matters in the legislature — this legislative interference in matters which ought not theoretically to be within the purview of the legislature — cannot be better described than in the words of the Fassett Committee in their report made in 1891 on the government of cities in the state of New York. "The situation then is as follows: That it is frequently impossible for the legislature, the municipal officers, or even for the courts, to tell what the laws mean; that it is usu-

---

[1] See Sanborn v. Rice County, 9 Minn. 273; People v. Hows, 37 Barb. 440; Plimpton v. Somerset, 33 Vt. 283; Gage v. Graham, 57 Ill. 144; State v. Tappan, 29 Wis. 664.

[2] In re Pennsylvania Hall, 5 Pa. St. 204; Borough of Dunmore's Appeal, 52 Pa. St. 374; Layton v. New Orleans, 12 La. Ann. 515. Compare Commonwealth v. Pittsburgh, 34 Pa. St. 496. In Vasser v. George, 47 Miss. 713, 720, Simrall, J., claims very broad authority for the legislature in adjusting claims against municipalities.

ally impossible for the legislature to tell what the probable effect of any alleged reform in the laws is likely to be; that it is impossible for any one, either in private life or in public office, to tell what the exact business condition of any city is, and that municipal government is a mystery even to the experienced; that municipal officers have no certainty as to their tenure of office; that municipal officers can escape responsibility for their acts or failures by securing amendments to the law; that municipal officers can escape responsibility to the public on account of the unintelligibility of the laws and the insufficient publicity of the facts relative to municipal government; that local authorities receive permission to increase the municipal debt for the performance of public works which should be paid for out of taxes; that the conflict of authority is sometimes so great as to result in a complete or partial paralysis of the service; that our cities have no real local autonomy; that local self-government is a misnomer, and that consequently so little interest is felt in matters of local business that in almost every city in the state it has fallen into the hands of professional politicians." [1]

This condition of things is attributed by the same body, "not only to the continued possibility

[1] *Senate Committee's Report*, Vol. V., p. 13.

of legislative interference, but" also to "the pertinacity with which interested parties or local authorities appeal to the legislature, year after year, in matters affecting city government, from the most important to the most insignificant, thus depriving the cities of their administrative autonomy, and subjecting them to conditions which do not prevail in the administration of the business of any other corporation whatever. For this the people are themselves very largely to blame, because of their indifference to the policy of their local authorities, and their failure to protect both themselves and the legislature by a knowledge and disclosure of the facts. These are conditions which, if applied to the business of any other corporation, would make the maintenance of a continued policy and a successful administration as impossible as they are to-day in the government of our municipalities, and produce waste and mismanagement such as is now the distinguishing feature of municipal business as compared with that of private corporations." [1]

The conception of the relation of the legislature to cities which has brought about these conditions [2] the courts have been powerless to correct,

[1] *Ibid.*
[2] Which is accurately expressed by the United States Supreme Court in the case of the United States *v.* The Baltimore and Ohio

except in one or two instances, on account of the indisputable powers of the legislature over municipal corporations. For these bodies have, except as to their property rights, no legal claim to protection under the general clauses in the American constitution guaranteeing private rights. At quite an early date in our history the United States Supreme Court intimated that municipal corporations, except so far as their property rights were concerned, were to be regarded as governmental agencies rather than as legal persons, and therefore subject to legislative regulation.[1]

In later times the same authority, in conjunction with the state courts, has held that a municipal charter is not a contract but merely a public legal privilege which may be amended by the legislature as it sees fit, and even taken away altogether.[2]

R. R. Co., 17 Wallace, 322, where it is said: "A municipal corporation . . . is a representative, not only of the state, but is a portion of its governmental power. It is one of its creatures made for a specific purpose, to exercise within the limited sphere, the powers of the state. The state may govern . . . the local territory as it governs the state at large. It may enlarge or contract its powers, or destroy its existence."

[1] Dartmouth College v. Woodward, 4 Wheaton, 518, 694.

[2] Meriwether v. Garrett, 102 U. S. 472, 511; Rogers v. Burlington, 3 Wallace, 654; New Orleans v. Clarke, 95 U. S. 644; Layton v. New Orleans, 12 La. Ann. 515; State v. B. & O. R. R. Co., 12 Gill & Johnson, Md. 399, affirmed in 3 Howard, U. S. 534.

The failure of the legislature in the exercise of its undoubted powers of control over municipal corporations to distinguish a sphere of municipal action in which they should move largely independently of central control, and its positive intrusion upon this sphere, are, while theoretically unjustifiable, at the same time excusable for several reasons. They are excusable in the first place because of the general system adopted in this country for the protection of private rights, to which reference is made in the next chapter.

CHAPTER III

THE EFFECT OF THE AMERICAN SYSTEM OF PROTECTING PRIVATE RIGHTS UPON THE ATTITUDE OF THE LEGISLATURE TOWARDS MUNICIPAL CORPORATIONS

"No feature in the government of the United States has awakened so much curiosity in the European mind, caused so much discussion, received so much admiration and been more frequently misunderstood than the duties assigned to the Supreme Court and the functions which it discharges in guarding the ark of the Constitution."[1]

"The success of this experiment has blinded men to its novelty. There is no exact precedent for it, either in the ancient or modern world. The builders of constitutions have, of course, foreseen the violation of constitutional rule, but they have generally sought for an exclusive remedy, not in the civil but in the criminal law,

---

[1] Bryce, *The American Commonwealth*, 1st American edition, Vol. I., p. 237.

through the impeachment of the offender; and in popular government, fear or jealousy of an authority not directly delegated by the people, has too often caused the difficulty to be left for settlement to chance, or to the arbitrament of arms."[1] The origin of this novel principle is to be found in the application of the ordinary principles of the English law, to the conditions existing in this country at the time of the formation of the first constitution. By the original English law, the courts had the power to inquire into the validity of the acts of the administration; and if such acts were found to be contrary to the law of the land, that is, the statutes of Parliament and custom as developed and formulated by the courts, they were recognized as possessing the power to declare such acts as invalid and to refuse to enforce them. At the time of the formation of the modern American government, and the organization of the separate states which afterwards together formed the United States, "the absolute authority of Parliament as sovereign was . . . transferred to the people, and the restraints which were applied to the executive in the English system became applicable to the new government as a whole."[2]

[1] Maine, *Popular Government*, p. 218.
[2] Elliot, "The Legislature and the Courts," in the *Political Science Quarterly*, Vol. V., p. 229.

Inasmuch as the constitution in all of the newly formed states contained, among other things, a bill of rights, that is an enumeration of the inalienable rights of the individual, of which it was provided in the constitution he might not be deprived by the action of any or all of the departments of the government, there was offered to him, through this enumeration, and through the power which the courts immediately obtained, and whose origin has already been described, an effectual guaranty that the sphere of freedom, which had been delimited in the constitution, should not be encroached upon. It is in these two particulars that the American system of delimiting the sphere of individual freedom of action, and of assuring an effectual guaranty that it will not be encroached upon, differs from the system provided in all other states. It is, indeed, true that the sphere of liberty which is recognized as belonging to the individual, is, in all modern states which have obtained constitutional government, essentially the same; but in all states outside of the United States, this sphere of individual freedom is rather the result of the act of the government than of that of the state. It is delimited by legislation rather than by the constitution, and, inasmuch as what has been done by the legislature may be changed by the legislature, the fact that a sphere of free individual action does elsewhere, as a matter of fact, exist, is, from a legal point of view, due entirely to the forbearance of that part of the government which has the power to delimit it, rather than to any positive inability on its part to encroach upon it.

While the American method of securing to the individual his sphere of freedom of action is undoubtedly the most efficacious that can be devised, it must be admitted that it has several important disadvantages. In the first place, it is extremely difficult at any given time to delimit a sphere of individual freedom which will be permanently satisfactory. As has been well said, "the elements of individual liberty cannot generally be stated for all states and for all times. All mankind is not to be found, or has not yet been found, upon the same stage of civilization. The individual liberty of the Russian would not suffice for the Englishman, nor that of the Englishman at the time of the Tudors for the Englishman of to-day." [1] Further, at any given time, private individuals are not only enjoying private rights which should not be interfered with by the government, but are also possessed of public privileges which are the legitimate objects of governmental

[1] Burgess, *Political Science and Comparative Constitutional Law*, Vol. I., p. 177.

control. For no greater mistake can be made than to suppose that the government, in either its central or local organizations, attends, or should attend, to all matters which are of public interest. The state attains its ends as well through liberty as through government, as well through entrusting the care of matters of public interest to individuals as through the maintenance of public governmental services for their management. But matters of public interest, which are entrusted to the care of private individuals, do not lose their public characteristics through the fact that they are thus attended to by private agencies. The state, therefore, should reserve to its governmental organization the power to control these matters where they are left in the care of individuals, so that they may be managed in the public interest, and not in that of the private persons who are permitted to attend to them. This has always been, in theory, the rule of the English common law, and is, at the present time, the doctrine of the United States Supreme Court, which recognizes that, notwithstanding that the constitution assures to the individual a large sphere of private rights, the state legislature still has a wide, perhaps too wide, police power, and that through the exercise of this police power the enjoyment of all public privileges by private individuals may be made to conform to the public interest.[1]

In former times the state looked on, with much more unconcern than at present, at the participation of private individuals or corporations in what is now considered governmental work, by their devotion of property to the furtherance of public interests. In the Middle Ages the Church, which has always been regarded among Christian peoples as a *quasi*-public corporation, attended to many matters which are now regarded as properly functions of the government. Such was the case with

---

[1] In the great case of Munn *v.* Illinois, 94 U. S., 113, Chief Justice Waite, in rendering the decision of the court, says: "This brings us to inquire as to the principles upon which this power of regulation rests, in order that we may determine what is within and what is without its operation. Looking then to the common law, from whence came the right which the constitution protects, we find that when private property is 'affected with a public interest, it ceases to be *juris privati* only.' This was said by Lord Chief Justice Hale more than 200 years ago, in his treatise *De Portibus Maris*, 1 Hargreave, *Legal Tracts*, p. 78, and has been accepted without objection, as an essential element of the law of property ever since. Property does become clothed with a public interest when used in a manner to make it of public consequence and affect the community at large. When, therefore, one devotes his property to a use in which the public has an interest, he, in effect, grants to the public an interest in that use, and must submit to be controlled by the public for the common good. He may withdraw his grant by discontinuing the use, but so long as he maintains the use, he must submit to the control." See also Barbier *v.* Connolly, 113 U. S. 27; Beer Co. *v.* Mass., 97 U. S. 659.

public charity and public education. With, however, the differentiation of the Church into denominations, based upon differences of religious belief in minor details, it has been found necessary, on account of the great influence which religion has upon such matters, for the government to take them into its immediate direction and control. The Church, which was at one time regarded as an organization of the government, has now been relegated very largely to the position of a private corporation.

It is extremely difficult to locate the line of demarcation between these public interests, managed by private corporations and private individuals and subject to governmental regulation and control, and private rights, in which the individual is to be protected against all encroachment upon the part of the government in any of its organizations. There is always danger that the domain of private right, which may be made practically unalterable by the constitution, may include not only private right but public privilege. If this is the case, there is danger of a return, partial, at any rate, to the feudal state. We have had several examples of this danger in our own history. Thus, for example, it has been decided that a relinquishment of the taxing power by the government, if the inducement to such relinquishment was in the nature of a consideration in the legal sense, is a contract, the obligation of which the government is then prevented from ever impairing.[1]

Another example is to be found in the decision that the legislature may not amend the charter of a private corporation, on the ground that such charter is a contract.[2] The public policy of such a decision is bad, and is seen to be so from the insertion in the constitutions of almost all the commonwealths, which have been adopted subsequent to this decision, of provisions which expressly allow the legislature to amend the charters of all corporations incorporated after the adoption of such constitutional provisions.

Such confusion of public privilege with private right is to be deprecated, for, since public privileges should be subject to governmental regulation, the community suffers very greatly if they are granted the same protection as private rights. The likelihood of such confusion is particularly great in the case of such bodies as municipal corporations which, as has been shown, are at the same time organizations for the satisfaction of local and *quasi*-private needs, and agencies of general state government. Such confusion is also

---

[1] See, for example, New Jersey *v.* Wilson, 7 Cranch, 164; Cooley, *Taxation*, 2d ed., 67; Burgess, *Political Science*, etc., Vol. I., p. 238.
[2] See Dartmouth College *v.* Woodward, 4 Wheaton, 636.

very disastrous in the case of these bodies. For if the domain of private rights is recognized at all, it may well happen that it be made to embrace as well certain governmental privileges, in which case the uniformity of administration of general matters may be destroyed, and the efficiency of the administration thereby greatly diminished.[1] If, on the other hand, the domain of public privilege is extended so as to include private and local rights, the administration of purely local matters is unduly centralized, and local government is destroyed.

In the second place, it must be admitted that the presence of a written constitution, containing an enumeration of the private rights of the individual, together with the power of the courts to declare void acts of the government encroaching upon them, has a tendency to relieve from responsibility the legislature, which is the organ of government in the United States from which the encroachment upon the sphere of individual freedom is mostly to be apprehended. The legislature gets to believe that private rights are to be protected by the courts, which have, without a doubt, shown themselves stout defenders of the sphere of free private action, and thus frequently attempts

---

[1] *E.g.*, see what is said in Chap. XII., p. 234, as to the effect of the administration of the English Poor Law by local bodies.

to exercise its powers with very little consideration for such rights, and passes a great many bills which really do encroach upon this sphere of individual liberty. A comparison of the action of the American legislature with that of the Parliament of England, where the courts are not regarded as having the power to protect the individual from the action of Parliament, even though subversive of his rights, is very instructive. The English Parliament, knowing that it alone is responsible for the protection of the sphere of individual liberty, is very chary about exercising its powers in such a way as to encroach upon them. No better example of this feeling of the English Parliament can be adduced than the discussion which occupied so largely the attention of the public at the time of the passage of the late local government bill of 1888, relative to the compensation of the owners of liquor licenses which were to be rendered less valuable than theretofore. Another good example of this extreme care for what are considered private rights is to be found in the usual provisions contained in all reform legislation for compensation to officers who may lose their places as a result of the changes proposed.[1] In this country both liquor licenses and public offices are considered by the constitutions as public privileges

[1] See Local Government Act, 1888, Secs. 20, 31.

and not private rights. They are, therefore, never protected by the courts,[1] nor does the legislature ever show them great consideration.

This habit which the American legislature gets into towards the private rights of individuals, because they are protected by the constitutions and the power of the courts to interpret the meaning of their provisions, becomes extremely disastrous when applied to individuals like municipal corporations, which, as we have seen, are not protected by the constitutions against the action of the legislature.

The fact that municipal corporations, although to a certain extent private in character, are still governmental institutions, and are, therefore, subject to the control of the legislature, when taken together with the habit of the legislature to regard the courts rather than itself as the protectors of private rights, has brought it about that the legislature in the exercise of its undoubted powers of control over municipal corporations has, as has been pointed out, forgotten in many instances that these bodies have private rights upon which the legislature ought not to encroach.

This centralization of local municipal functions in the hands of the legislature has been caused,

---

[1] Metropolitan Board of Excise v. Barrie, 34 N. Y. 657; Butler v. Pennsylvania, 10 How. U. S. 402.

however, not simply by the system adopted in America of protecting private rights. It is also in part a result, and a natural result, of the rule that has been adopted in our law as to the extent of the municipal powers which are ordinarily to be found in our city charters.

CHAPTER IV

THE EFFECTS OF THE RULE OF THE AMERICAN LAW AS TO MUNICIPAL POWERS UPON THE ATTITUDE OF THE LEGISLATURE TOWARDS MUNICIPAL CORPORATIONS

LEGISLATIVE action with regard to municipal affairs has been necessary and unavoidable as a result of the narrow powers with reference to municipal affairs, which the law recognizes are possessed by municipal corporations. No better or more authoritative statement of the powers ordinarily possessed by municipal corporations can be found than that given by Judge Dillon in his great work on municipal corporations, and approved by many of the later decisions of the courts themselves. He says: "It is a general and undisputed proposition of law that a *municipal corporation possesses and can exercise the following powers and no others.* First, those granted in *express words;* second, those *necessarily or fairly implied* in or *incident* to the powers expressly granted; third, those *essential* to the declared objects and purposes of the corporations not simply convenient, but indispensable. Any fair reasonable doubt concerning the existence of power is resolved by the courts against the corporation and the power is denied. Of every municipal corporation the charter or statute by which it is created is its organic act. Neither the corporation nor its officers can do any act or make any contract or incur any liability not authorized thereby, or by some legislative act applicable thereto. All acts beyond the scope of the powers granted are void."[1] Judge Dillon adds that while the rule "of strict construction of corporate powers is not so directly applicable to the ordinary clauses in the charters or incorporating acts of municipalities as it is to the charters of private corporations . . . it is equally applicable to grants of powers to municipal and public bodies which are out of the usual range, or which may result in public burdens, or which, in their exercise, touch the right to liberty or property, or, as it may be compendiously expressed, any common-law right of the citizen, or inhabitant."[2] The necessary result of such a rule of law, with the accompanying strict construction which is usual, is that the municipalities will often apply to the source of authority, that is the legis-

[1] Dillon, *Law of Municipal Corporations*, 4th ed., p. 145.
[2] *Ibid.*, p. 148.

lature, for an increase of power in order that any doubt as to the existence of particular powers, which it is desired to exercise but which are not clearly conferred by the charter, may be dissipated. This condition of things has been aggravated by the fact that originally in this country all city charters were to be found in special acts, the passage of which with their amendments necessitated frequent action by the legislature with regard not only to municipal affairs generally, but with regard to the municipal affairs of particular cities. A recent case, however,[1] shows a decided tendency to depart from this rule of enumerated powers and their strict construction, and to recognize as existing in municipal corporations from the mere fact of their incorporation a very large range of powers over purely local matters. In this case the question that arose was whether the municipal corporation had the right to establish an electric lighting plant, not only for the lighting of the streets of the city, but also for the distribution of the electric light among the inhabitants. The only statute bearing upon the question was a general one providing that the common council of any city might light the streets and other public places of the city with the electric light, and might contract

[1] City of Crawfordsville v. Braden, 130 Indiana, 149, 30 American State Reports, 214.

with any individuals or corporations for lighting such streets and other public places, or for granting to any person or corporation the right to erect and maintain in the streets the necessary poles and appliances for the purpose of supplying the electric light to the inhabitants of the corporation. The only reference to the power of distributing the electric light among the inhabitants of the corporation was the one granting the power to make a contract for such a purpose with some private corporation. The court, however, put aside altogether this specific provision of law upon the subject of electric lighting which would not seem to authorize the city to distribute the electric light. It did this notwithstanding the general rule that the enumeration of specific powers prevents a body to which such specific powers are granted from exercising other similar powers, and based itself upon the implied powers which result from the incorporation of a municipality. Among these implied powers, the court held, is the power to enact and enforce reasonable by-laws and ordinances for the protection of health, life, and property. This general police power, it was held, gave the power to light the streets and the public places independently of any specific statutory power to that effect. The power to light the streets, it was held, gave the power to determine as to what was the best method of lighting the streets. After having thus proved that the city possessed the power to light the streets by electricity, the court goes on to say: "We can see no good reason why it may not also at the same time furnish it [the electric light] to the inhabitants to light their residences and places of business. To do so is, in our opinion, a legitimate exercise of the police power for the preservation of property and health."

This declaration, if generally followed, will be far-reaching in its effects. For if we may derive from the mere fact of incorporation the power to distribute electric light among the inhabitants of the municipality, notwithstanding the existence of a specific statute with regard to electric light, which merely grants the power to the municipality to contract with a private corporation for this purpose, it is difficult to see what powers of a local character are not possessed by a municipal corporation, either as the result of the mere fact of its incorporation or as the result of the general grant of police power which is often contained in a city charter or a general incorporation act. Frequent resort to the legislature by municipal corporations for increase of power will not be necessary.

But whatever may be in theory the material powers, *i.e.* the powers to undertake municipal services, recognized as possessed by municipal corporations as a result of the fact of their incorporation, or as incident to the general police powers which they often have, their exercise is in all cases very largely dependent upon the extent of the financial powers of these bodies — *i.e.* their powers to raise money. If they have narrow financial powers, the widest material powers are of little value, and resort will have to be had to the source of authority, the legislature, to increase these financial powers, in order that their material powers may be put into execution.

What now are the common-law financial powers of municipal corporations? The sources from which municipal corporations may derive revenue are three in number: viz., property, taxes, assessments and licenses, and loans. So far as the first is concerned, all that need be said is that, by the common law, municipal corporations may acquire in the usual way and hold property for any purpose germane to the purpose of their incorporation.[1] As a necessary result they may receive the income coming from such property, and may appropriate it to any corporate purpose where it is not affected by a trust of some sort.

As to the second, however, no municipal corpo-

---

[1] McDonough's Executors *v.* Murdock, 15 Howard, 363; Ketchum *v.* Buffalo, 14 N. Y. 356; Dillon, *Municipal Corporations*, 4th ed., Chap. XV.

ration may, in the absence of special authorization by the legislature, levy any tax,[1] and such special authorization often limits the rate of taxation which may be imposed. Further, even the general authority which is ordinarily contained in a city charter to levy taxes will not authorize the laying of assessments.[2] It would seem, also, that incidental revenue at any rate may be derived from licenses, and indeed from the general exercise of police powers.[3]

In the third place, while there seems to be little doubt that a municipal corporation may, without special legislative authority and as a result of the exercise of its contractual powers, incur indebtedness to be paid out of the ordinary income for the current year,[4] there is considerable doubt as to its power without such authority to borrow money.[5] Even more doubtful is its power, under similar conditions, to issue negotiable paper or bonds in evidence of its debts.[6] But whatever may be the power of municipal corporations to borrow money or issue negotiable bonds without legislative au-

---

[1] Cooley, *Taxation*, 2d ed., p. 329, and cases cited.
[2] *Ibid.*, p. 609.
[3] *Ibid.*, Chap. XIX., p. 586.
[4] Nashville *v.* Ray, 19 Wallace, 468.
[5] *Ibid.* But see Williamsport *v.* Com., 84 Pa. St. 487, 24 Amer. Dec. 208.
[6] City of Brenham *v.* German American Bank, 144 U. S. 173.

thority, as a matter of fact, the legislature has been in this particular very prodigal in its grants of the necessary power, perhaps more so than its grants of the taxing power. The report of the Fassett Committee says: "Local authorities receive permission to increase the municipal debt for the performance of public works which should be paid for out of taxes."[1] It has in some cases not only granted the power, but even has forced municipalities to incur debts, and that too for purposes not of a municipal character; as, *e.g.*, to aid railroads.[2] So careless has the legislature been in this respect that it has been necessary for the people of the states to take the matter in hand, and to provide in the constitution that municipal corporations shall not incur debts for any purposes beyond a certain amount,— generally a percentage of the assessment roll,— nor any debts at all in aid of any private corporations such as railroad companies.[3]

These constitutional provisions do not, however, increase the financial powers of municipal corporations. These powers remain as they were before, practically, at any rate, very narrow in the

[1] Report, Vol. V., p. 14.

[2] See Perkins *v.* Slack, 86 Pa. St. 283; People *v.* Batchellor, 53 N. Y. 128; Duanesburgh *v.* Jenkins, 57 N. Y. 177; Cooley, *Taxation*, p. 699.

[3] See, *e.g.*, Const. of New York, Art. VIII., Sec. 10.

absence of specific legislative action. For bonds cannot be placed on the market, or money borrowed to any advantage, if there is any doubt as to the authority to make the loan. When we consider this fact in connection with the narrow common-law material powers of municipalities, we must admit that the relation of the legislature to municipal corporations has in the past been such as not only to encourage, but even to necessitate frequent special action by the legislature relative to municipal affairs.

Finally, when it is remembered that one of the characteristics of American municipal development, of the larger cities at any rate, is the constant emphasizing of the public character of the cities through the conferring upon them by the legislature of functions of general administration, it will at once be seen how easy, indeed how really unavoidable, has been the confusion on the part of the legislatures as to local and public matters. For the more public the character of the city, the greater will be the actual necessity for the legislature to interfere with the city government. This is required in the interest of the state as a whole, certain of whose affairs are, where the position of the city is public in character, being attended to by the city government. The experience of the city of New York is an illustration of this fact. New

York is a county as well as a city. New York has therefore to discharge all the public governmental functions elsewhere in the state discharged by the county; and no city in the state of New York has suffered as much from special legislation.[1] The frequency of actually necessary special action with reference to cities, resulting from their public position, increases the temptation of the legislature to interfere where its interference is not only unnecessary, but even pernicious.

Being called upon continually to enlarge the extent of municipal powers, being at the same time obliged to exercise a central control over matters of general concern attended to by cities, and generally feeling, for the reasons adduced, little responsibility for the protection of private and local rights, the legislature has easily confused its powers of authorization with its powers of compulsion, and has exercised the latter where it should have confined itself to the exercise of the former. It has come to regulate itself local matters, and has encroached upon the domain of municipal home rule. This encroachment upon the field of local self-government has been productive of greater evil than its attempted encroachments on the domain

---

[1] *Supra*, p. 23, as to the great amount of special legislation with reference to New York.

of the rights of private individuals. For, while the courts could protect individual private rights, they have been unable to protect the rights of local government of municipal corporations.

CHAPTER V

THE CONSTITUTIONAL LIMITATIONS OF THE POWER OF THE LEGISLATURE OVER MUNICIPAL AFFAIRS

THE undoubted and well-recognized evils of the American system of controlling municipal corporations, with the resulting continual legislative interference in purely local matters, have caused us, in the United States, to resort to the remedy to which we had before resorted, in order to protect the sphere of freedom of private individuals. That is, we have incorporated into most of our later state constitutions, provisions which limit very largely the power of the legislature to interfere with the affairs of municipal corporations. In twenty states, the legislature is forbidden by the constitution to incorporate cities, and generally also villages, by special act. These are Arkansas,[1] California,[2] Illinois,[3] Indiana,[4] Iowa,[5] Kansas,[6] Ken-

---

[1] Constitution, XII., Sec. 3.
[2] Constitution, XI., Sec. 6.
[3] Constitution, IV., Sec. 22.
[4] Constitution, XI., Sec. 13.
[5] Constitution, III., Sec. 30.
[6] Constitution, XII., Sec. 1.

tucky,[1] Louisiana,[2] Mississippi,[3] Missouri,[4] Nebraska,[5] North Dakota,[6] Ohio,[7] Pennsylvania,[8] South Dakota,[9] Tennessee,[10] Washington,[11] West Virginia,[12] Wisconsin,[13] and Wyoming.[14] In the states of Minnesota[15] and Texas[16] the legislature is forbidden by the constitution to incorporate by special act, in the one case, towns and villages, in the other, cities and towns of less than ten thousand inhabitants. Of these twenty states, twelve, namely, Illinois, Louisiana, Missouri, Nebraska, North Dakota, Pennsylvania, South Dakota, Texas, Washington, West Virginia, Wisconsin, and Wyoming apply the prohibition of special legislation as well to amendments or changes in the charters of the corporations which they affect, as to the original incorporation of such bodies. Generally, however, such amendments are regarded by the courts as coming within the general prohibition of special

---

[1] Constitution, Secs. 59, 17, and Sec. 56.

[2] Constitution, Sec. 46. This excepts the city of New Orleans and levee districts and parishes.

[3] Constitution, Sec. 178.

[4] Constitution, IV., Sec. 53.

[5] Constitution, III., Sec. 15.

[6] Constitution, Sec. 69, p. 33.

[7] Constitution, XIII., Secs. 1, 6.

[8] Constitution, III., Sec. 7.

[9] Constitution, III., Sec. 23.

[10] Constitution, XI., Sec. 1.

[11] Constitution, II., Sec. 28, par. 8.

[12] Constitution, VI., Sec. 39.

[13] Constitution, Amendment IV., Sec. 31.

[14] Constitution, III., Sec. 27.

[15] Constitution, IV., Sec. 3, par. 7, 9.

[16] Constitution, XI., Secs. 4, 5.

incorporation acts. In the cases of Indiana, Louisiana, New Jersey, and Tennessee, the prohibition is expressed against the conferring of corporate powers generally by special act. Such provisions are generally regarded as including within their limitation municipal as well as private corporations.[1] There seems to be some doubt, however, as to whether such provisions will apply to *quasi*-municipal corporations, such as school districts, as well as to municipal corporations proper.[2] Certain of the states, seventeen in number, among which are to be included some of those prohibiting special incorporation acts, require the legislature specifically to pass general acts for the incorporation of municipalities. These are Arkansas,[3] California,[4] Colorado,[5] Idaho,[6] Iowa,[7] Kansas,[8] Kentucky,[9] Missouri,[10] New Jersey,[11] North

---

[1] Thus in the case of Purdy *v.* The People, 4 Hill, 384, it was held that a constitutional provision requiring a two-thirds majority for the passage of any act affecting any body, politic or corporate, applied as well to public as to private corporations. See also State *v.* Newark, 40 N. J. Law, 550, 558.

[2] See Beach *v.* Leahy, 11 Kansas, 25, which holds that *quasi* corporations are not included within the prohibition, and Clegg *v.* Richardson County, 8 Nebraska, 178; Dundy *v.* Richardson County, 8 Nebraska, 508, which hold to the contrary rule.

[3] XII., Sec. 3.
[4] XI., Sec. 6.
[5] XIV., Sec. 13.
[6] XII., Sec. 1.
[7] VIII., Sec. 1.
[8] XII., Sec. 5.
[9] Sec. 56.
[10] IX., Sec. 7.
[11] IV., Sec. VII, par. 11. The constitution of New Jersey pro-

Dakota,[1] Ohio,[2] South Dakota,[3] Texas, in case of cities and towns of less than ten thousand inhabitants,[4] Washington,[5] West Virginia,[6] Wisconsin,[7] and Wyoming.[8]

Further, in quite a number of states, among which are to be included some of those already mentioned, the legislature is also forbidden by the constitution to regulate, by special act, the internal affairs of the localities or certain of the localities. Generally this provision applies only to counties and towns. These commonwealths are California,[9] Colorado,[10] Idaho,[11] Illinois,[12] Indiana,[13] Missouri,[14] Montana,[15] Nebraska,[16] Nevada,[17] New Jersey,[18] North Dakota,[19] Pennsylvania,[20] South

---

vides that the legislature shall pass general laws under which corporations may be organized, and corporate powers of every nature obtained. This was the provision which was construed by the case of State v. Newark, cited above.

[1] Article VI.
[2] XIII., Sec. 6.
[3] X., Sec. 1.
[4] XI., Secs. 4, 5.
[5] XI., Sec. 10.
[6] XI., Sec. 1. This affects all corporations.
[7] Amendment IV., Sec. 32.
[8] XIII. In Wyoming, the consent of the majority of the electors is required for the incorporation of any district as a municipality.
[9] IV., Sec. 25, par. 9.
[10] IV., Sec. 25.
[11] III., Sec. 19.
[12] IV., Sec. 22.
[13] IV., Sec. 22.
[14] All localities, IV., Sec. 53.
[15] VI., Sec. 26.
[16] III., Sec. 15.
[17] IV., Sec. 20.
[18] IV., Sec. 7, par. 11.
[19] II., Sec. 69, par. 4 and 32.
[20] All localities, III., Sec. 7.

Dakota,[1] Texas,[2] West Virginia,[3] and Wyoming.[4]

Still further in other states, the constitution assures to the localities the right of local government, either by forbidding the legislature to provide by special act for local offices or commissions to regulate local affairs, or by giving the people of all or certain of the localities the right to select all or certain local officers.[5]

Finally, in quite a number of instances, specific actions upon the part of the legislature are either forbidden altogether, or the legislature is forbidden to act in these instances by special act. For example, in California,[6] Washington,[7] and Illinois,[8] the legislature may not impose taxes on municipal

---

[1] III., Sec. 23, par. 4.   [3] VI., Sec. 39.
[2] All localities. III., Sec. 56.   [4] III., Sec. 27.
[5] Of these the most important are: California, IV., Sec. 25, par. 9. XI., Sec. 11; Colorado, V., Sec. 35; Idaho, III., Sec. 19, XVIII., Sec. 19; Illinois, IV., Sec. 22, X., Secs. 6 and 8; Indiana, IV., Sec. 22, VI., Secs. 1 to 3; Kansas, IX.; Kentucky, Secs. 97 to 99 and 160; Maryland, IV., Sec. 44, VII., Sec. 1; Michigan, X., Sec. 3, XI., XV., Sec. 14; Minnesota, XI., Sec. 4; Mississippi, VI., Secs. 170 and 171; Montana, V., Secs. 26 and 36, XVI., Secs. 4 to 6; Nebraska, III., Sec. 15, X., Sec. 4; Nevada, IV., Secs. 20 and 26; New Jersey, IV., Sec. 7, par. 11; New York, X., Secs. 1 and 2; North Dakota, II., Sec. 69, par. 32; Ohio, X.; Pennsylvania, III., Secs. 7 and 20, V., Sec. 11, XIV., XV., Sec. 2; South Dakota, IX.; Texas, III., Sec. 56; Virginia, VI., Secs. 15 to 20; Washington, XI., Sec. 5; West Virginia, IX.; Wyoming, III., Sec. 27, XII., Sec. 5.
[6] XII., Sec. 12.   [7] XI., Sec. 10.   [8] XIX., Sec. 10.

corporations, or the inhabitants thereof, or on their property for corporate purposes. In quite a number of states also, the legislature may not divide counties or change the county seats, without the consent of the people.¹ It is very commonly provided also that the legislature may not, by special act, open or vacate streets or highways. In three of the states, in addition to thus prohibiting special legislation, the constitution provides that cities of a certain size shall have the power to frame their own charters and amend them, such charters and amendments being in all cases, however, subject to the constitution of the state and the general laws.²

In quite a number of the states the abuses resulting from the grant by the legislature, by special act or otherwise, of street franchises, have been stopped, either by requiring the consent of the local authorities to the grant or absolutely prohibiting the grant by special laws. In most cases these constitutional provisions affect merely the grant of the right to a corporation to use the streets for the purposes of railways, either horse railways or steam railways.³ In Rhode Island, it is remark-

---

[1] See Illinois, X., Sec. 2 ; Idaho, XVIII., Sec. 3 ; Colorado, XIV., Sec. 3; Iowa, III., Sec. 30 ; Kansas, XIX., Sec. 1 ; Kentucky, Sec. 64 ; Arkansas, XIII.

[2] These states are: Missouri, XIX., Sec. 7; California, XI., Secs. 6 to 8; Washington, XI., Sec. 10.

[3] These states are: Colorado, V., Sec. 25, XV., Sec. 11, which

able that Article IX. of the Constitutional Amendments requires that the grant of the right to use the streets shall be made by special law.

These constitutional provisions do not, indeed, so much attempt to limit the regulative power of the legislature over municipal corporations as to insist upon its exercise in a particular manner. At the same time their indirect effect is very greatly to strengthen the position of municipal corporations over against the legislature; for the prohibition of special laws often prevents the legislature from interfering in matters of purely local concern affecting some particular municipal corporation, and really obliges it to delegate much

both prohibits special legislation and provides for the consent of the local authorities in all cases; Idaho, XI., Sec. 11, which requires merely the consent of the local authorities; Illinois, IV., Sec. 22, XI., Sec. 4, both prohibiting special law and requiring consent; Kentucky, Sec. 59, par. 19, Sec. 163, which affects street franchises generally, prohibiting both special law and requiring the consent of the local authorities; Louisiana, Article 46, prohibiting all special acts, unless notice is given in the locality; Mississippi, Sec. 90, prohibiting all special acts; Missouri, IV., Sec. 53, prohibiting special acts; Montana, VI., Sec. 26, prohibiting special acts; Nebraska, III., Sec. 15, XIII., Sec. 2, prohibiting special acts requiring consent of the local authorities; New Jersey, Art. IV., Sec. VII, p. 11, prohibiting special acts; North Dakota, II., Sec. 69, par. 20, prohibiting special acts; Pennsylvania, III., Sec. 7, prohibiting special acts; South Dakota, Art. X., Sec. 3, street franchises generally; Wyoming, XIII., Sec. 4, III., Sec. 27, relating to street franchises generally, both requiring consent and prohibiting special acts.

greater powers than it otherwise would delegate to local bodies. In some instances, however, all action on the part of the legislature is forbidden; as, for example, in the case of the provisions insuring the localities the right to elect their own officers. The exact degree of limitation upon the power of the legislature over the localities that results from these constitutional provisions, can be determined only by the answer to two questions: First, what is a special act under the constitution; and, second, what are the corporate powers which may not be conferred by special act, or what are the affairs or the internal affairs of the corporation which may not be regulated by special act.

I. *What is a Special Act?*

The recent constitution of New York is the only one which specifically defines a special act. Such an act is said to be an act affecting less than all the cities of one of the classes of cities for which the constitution provides. In all the other commonwealths what is a special act is determined by the courts in their construction of the constitution.

It is to be noticed here, in the first place, that the courts do not hold themselves precluded from investigating facts by the passage by the legislature, of an act which is general in form, but which is actually special in its application. The Illinois constitution forbids the legislature to pass special laws regulating county and township affairs. In the case of Devine *v.* Cook County [1] it was held that an act applying to counties of over one hundred thousand inhabitants whose purpose was to erect a court-house, jail, and other public buildings for the use of such county, and to fund the floating debt of the county, — the act referring to the recent destruction of such buildings by fire, — was unconstitutional. In this case the duration of the law was for six years, and the court, in giving its opinion, said : —

"Its very terms preclude it from having any application to any county except the county of Cook ; for we take judicial notice no other county in this state contains over one hundred thousand inhabitants, nor can it be expected by any ordinary influx or increase of population, that any other county will have that population within the brief period fixed for the duration of this law, namely, within a period of six years from the time the act should take effect." While this case is one of the few which expressly lays down the principle that the courts will take judicial notice of the facts surrounding the act, almost

[1] 84 Illinois, 590.

all the decisions which the courts have been called upon to make in construction of these constitutional provisions, are really based upon this principle. On the other hand, the courts do not attempt to prevent the legislature from classifying municipal corporations. It is explicitly declared in many cases that, notwithstanding the existence of a constitutional provision prohibiting the legislature from regulating municipal affairs by special act, the legislature may still classify municipal corporations. This rule has been adopted, because it is believed to be practically impossible to pass one general law which can be applied with advantage to all the municipalities of the state. In every state there is usually at least one city whose institutions, resulting from its situation, are so peculiar as to make it almost impossible to apply to it a rule which may be applied with advantage to the cities of the state as a whole. In some cases the dangers of such a Procrustean procedure of applying the same rule to all cases are recognized in the constitution itself, which expressly permits the legislature to classify, as it sees fit, the cities for which a general municipal incorporation act is required.[1]

---

[1] This is true in Arkansas, XII., Sec. 2; Idaho, XII., Sec. 1; Washington, XI., Sec. 10. In several other states, classification is permitted, but is limited to either four or six classes. This is so in

The dangers inherent in the absolute prohibition of all special legislation are largely avoided also by the method adopted in Missouri, California, and Washington, where, as has been pointed out, cities of a certain size have the power to frame their own charters. They completely disappear also under the system of securing municipal home rule adopted in the recent constitution of New York, which provides merely for a suspensive veto to be exercised after a public hearing by the municipal authorities, of cities affected, upon all special legislation relating to municipal property, affairs, or government.[1]

But while the courts, where no limitations of the power of the legislature to classify municipal corporations are to be found in the constitution, permit such classification, they insist that the classification which shall be adopted must be based upon the varying necessities of the various municipal corporations within the state. Thus in the case of State v. Hammer,[2] the court says: "The marks of distinction on which the classification is founded must be such, in the nature of things, as will, in some reasonable way at least,

---

Colorado, XIV., Sec. 13; Kentucky, Sec. 156, permitting six classes, and fixing the classes itself; South Dakota, X., Sec. 1, and Wyoming, XIII., Sec. 1.

[1] N. Y. Const., XII., sec. 2.   [2] 42 N. J. Law, 485.

account for or justify the restriction of the legislature." The court goes on to give an example of legitimate classification, which is found in a law that should give to all cities in the state situated on tide water, the privilege of using such water in connection with sewers. "In such an enactment, but a part of the cities of the state would be embraced, but the classification would be lawful and proper, inasmuch as the places embraced would be possessed of a characteristic distinct from those possessed by the excluded places, such characteristic being of such a nature as to afford a reasonable ground for such special legislation."

Another instance of a proper basis of classification is to be found in Bronson v. Oberlin.[1] In this case it was held that under a constitutional provision which prohibited the legislature from granting corporate powers by special act, it was perfectly proper for the legislature to pass an act affecting only all incorporated villages "having within their limits a college or a university," inasmuch as the presence of such a college or university might give to the village a characteristic which was peculiar to itself. In this particular case, the act attempted to regulate matters connected with excise administration. In the case of Van Riper v. Parsons[2] this principle was carried still further.

[1] 41 Ohio St., 476. [2] 40 N. J. Law, 123.

Here it was held that an act to repeal all acts which gave to the Senate and General Assembly in joint meeting the appointment of commissioners to regulate municipal affairs, was valid, notwithstanding the fact that it applied to only one city; and the court said, in rendering its opinion: "The law in all its provisions is general, broad enough to reach every portion of the state, and abating legislative commissions for the regulation of municipal affairs, wherever they existed. Such commissions are distinguished from other sorts of municipal governments by characteristics sufficiently marked and important to make them clearly a class by themselves, and upon the whole of this class this law operates equally by force of terms which are restricted to no locality. A law so framed is not a special or local, but a general, law, without regard to the consideration that within the state there happens to be but one individual of the class or one place where it produces effects."

Population, also, has been held to be a proper basis of classification, even if through its application as a means of classification only one individual is to be found in a class at the time it is made. Thus, it has been held that a law putting cities of over three hundred thousand inhabitants in a single class was perfectly constitutional, although only one city in the state was in the class; and the court said, in rendering its opinion: "Legislation is intended not only to meet the wants of the present, but to provide for the future; it deals not with the past, but in theory at least, anticipates the needs of a state healthy with a vigorous development. It is intended to be permanent. At no distant day, Pittsburgh will probably become a city of the first class. . . . In the meantime, is the classification as to cities of the first class bad because Philadelphia is the only one of the class? We think not. Classification does not depend upon numbers. The first man, Adam, was as distinctly a class when the breath of life was breathed into him as at any subsequent period. The word is used not to designate numbers, but the rank or order of persons or things; in society it is used to indicate equality, or persons distinguished by common characteristics; as, the trading classes, the laboring classes; in science, it is a division or arrangement containing subordinate divisions of order, genus, or species." [1]

The point brought out in the case of Wheeler v. Philadelphia, namely, that a classification which

---

[1] Judge Paxson, who renders the opinion of the court, says that if the classification of cities is not regarded as constitutional, certain cities will be deprived of all means of development. Wheeler v. Philadelphia, 77 Pa. St. 338.

has reference rather to the future than the present, is perfectly proper, even though at the time that it is made only one city will be contained within a given class, is emphasized in the case of State *v.* Pugh.[1] In this case, an act was passed, purporting to affect cities of the first grade of the second class, but actually affecting only one city, to wit, Columbus; and the court said, in rendering its decision, and basing itself upon its previous decisions: "It is not to be urged against legislation general in form concerning cities of a designated class or grade, that but one city in the state is within the particular classification at the time of the enactment, nor is it fatal to the act in question that the belief or intent of the individual members of the General Assembly, who voted for the act was, that it should apply only to a particular city. . . . Although it is . . . admitted . . . that no other city than Columbus is within . . . the class and grade contemplated by the act, yet if any other city may in the future by virtue of its increase in population, and the action of its municipal authorities, ripen into a city of the same class and grade, and come within the operation of the act, it is still a law of a general nature, and is not invalid, even if it confer corporate powers. On the other hand, if it is clear that

[1] 43 Ohio St. 98.

no other city in the state can in the future come within its operation without doing violence to the manifest object and purpose of its enactment, and to the clear legislative intent, it is a local and special act, however strongly the form it is made to assume may suggest its general character."

The courts do not, however, permit the legislature to provide for a classification of cities or counties even by population where such classification is designed to operate in the present and on an existing state of facts, and not in the future, and even if several localities are actually in the class as formed. Thus, where the constitution provides that the legislature shall not pass local or special laws regulating the affairs of counties and cities, it has been held that an act providing for the establishment at once of a reform school in all counties having a city of over fifty thousand inhabitants is void if it apply to only one county.[1] A similar case is that of State *v.* Hermann.[2] Here an act provided that the Governor should "appoint and commission, in all cities having a population of one hundred thousand inhabitants or more, one notary public only to every three thousand inhabitants." In another section the act provided that all acts inconsistent with it were repealed, and that the office

---

[1] State *v.* The County Court of Jackson County, 89 Missouri, 237.
[2] 75 Missouri, 340.

of every notary public in such city who held a commission bearing date prior to the passage of the act, and whose term of office had not expired at the time the act became a law, should be abolished. The act was held unconstitutional.[1] Again, in Pennsylvania, where the constitution prohibits local or special laws touching the affairs of cities and counties, an act was declared void which regulated the pay and duties of certain officers in counties having between one hundred thousand and one hundred and fifty thousand inhabitants. Though four counties were affected, the act was so framed as to apply only in the present, and not to affect other counties whose future population might bring them within its scope.[2] Another case to the same effect is that of Topeka v. Gillette.[3] Here an act applied to three cities in the state and allowed such cities only fourteen days to begin, and fifty-eight days to complete, action under it. It was held that such a statute was void under a constitutional provision forbidding the legislature to confer corporate powers by special act. In this case the court said: "For the purposes of this act we shall assume that the legislature may pass valid

---

[1] See also State v. Township Committee of Northampton, 14 Atlantic Reporter, 587.

[2] McCarthy v. Commonwealth, 110 Penn. St. 243.

[3] 32 Kansas, 431.

acts concerning corporate powers, where the acts themselves for the time being apply only to one municipal corporation, as, for instance, the various acts passed by the legislature of Kansas from 1862 to 1880 for the government of cities of the first class, and which acts really applied only to the single city of Leavenworth. But such acts, in order to be valid, must in their form be general, and they must also be such that in the ordinary course of things they might, and probably would, apply to other corporations. Take, for instance, of the first class of cities the act that was first enacted in this state. That act was for the government of all cities or municipal corporations of not less than seven thousand inhabitants (law of 1863, chapter 46). At the time of its passage it applied only to the single city of Leavenworth, but it was a general act in its form, theoretically applying to a class of cities and theoretically enacted for all time to come, and if it had not been repealed or modified by subsequent legislation it would now apply to nine different cities in the state of Kansas. Theoretically, it was enacted for all cities which might in all the future attain to a population of seven thousand as well as for the city of Leavenworth, which then had that population. If, however, at the time of its passage there had been no probability that any other city in the state of

Kansas than Leavenworth would ever attain a population of seven thousand, the act in all probability would long ago have been declared unconstitutional and void as being a special act."

This last-mentioned constitutional provision was likewise the ground of a decision that it was improper for the legislature to pass an act referring to cities by name; as, for example, an act that "the cities of Osage, Mission, Wichita, Council Grove, and the town of Sabetha in Nemaha County, shall be constituted cities of the second class."[1] It has also been held that, under a constitutional provision prohibiting the legislature from passing any special or local law regulating the internal affairs of towns and counties, an act was unconstitutional which applied to all cities of the second class in which there was a city physician.[2]

Finally, the courts, by the great weight of authority, have held that classification, according to geographical conditions, is improper under constitutional provisions prohibiting special legislation, on the ground that geographical conditions are permanent, and that accordingly any act which at the beginning of its application is special in character must always remain so, and is, there-

---

[1] City of Council Grove, 20 Kansas, 619.

[2] State v. Simon, decided in the courts of New Jersey and reported in 22 Atlantic Reporter, 120.

fore, unconstitutional. The strongest case upon this point is that of the Commonwealth *v.* Patton.[1] Here an act was passed which provided "That in all counties of this commonwealth where there is a population of more than sixty thousand inhabitants, and in which there shall be any city incorporated at the time of the passage of this act, with a population exceeding eight thousand inhabitants, situated at a distance from the county seat of more than twenty-seven miles by the usually travelled public road, it shall be the duty of the president judge, and of the additional law judge, or either, to make an order providing for the holding of one week of court after each regular term of court for said county, for the trial of civil and criminal cases in said city." On an application for a *mandamus* to compel the commissioners of the county affected by the act to provide suitable buildings for the courts, it was decided that the *mandamus* could not issue, as the act referred to was special in character and contrary to a constitutional provision forbidding the legislature to pass any special or local law regulating the affairs of counties and townships. In delivering the opinion of the court, Chief Justice Paxson says: "This is classification run mad. Why not say all counties named Crawford, with a population exceeding sixty thousand

---

[1] 88 Penn. St., 258.

inhabitants, that contain a city called Titusville, with a population of over eight thousand inhabitants, situate twenty-seven miles from the county seat? Or all counties with a population of over sixty thousand, watered by a certain river or bounded by a certain mountain? There can be no proper classification of cities or counties, except by population. The moment we resort to geographical distinctions we enter the domain of special legislation, for the reason that such classification operates upon certain cities and counties to the perpetual exclusion of all others.... That is not classification which merely designates one county in the commonwealth and contains no provision by which any other county may by reason of its increase of population in the future come within one class."

To a similar effect is the decision in the case of State v. Philbrick.[1] Here an act referring exclusively to boroughs which are sea-side resorts was held unconstitutional, the court saying, "Contiguity to sea is no ground for the existence of a different rule in respect to the general amount of taxes to be raised [the act affected the method of raising taxes], and I am clear that no reason can be suggested why the power to designate the

[1] Decided in the courts of New Jersey and reported in 15 Atlantic Reporter, 579.

amount should, in boroughs not lying on the ocean, be committed to the people at large, while in boroughs on the sea the power should be placed in the hands of commissioners." [1]

Another good instance of the care the courts take to prevent the legislature from nullifying these constitutional provisions is to be found in a late case decided in New Jersey.[2] Here it was held that an act originally general in character, which, at the time of its passage, applied to no city (thus an act applying nominally to every city which contained within its limits more than two assembly districts completely and exclusively within its limits, and embracing no territory outside of the city), and is made by a subsequent act to apply to only one city (as, for example, an act rearranging assembly districts so that there was only one city which had, within its limits, two or more such assembly districts), becomes special in character, and is void.

II. *What are Municipal Affairs?*

A consideration of the cases which have been decided, relative to this question, will lead to the

---

[1] See also the case of Clark *v.* Cape May, 14 Atlantic Reporter, 581, which referred to sea-side boroughs and adopted a different method for the organization of their police force.

[2] State *v.* Mayor, 20 Atlantic Reporter, 886.

conclusion that to the courts which have been called upon to consider the matter, the special character of the act involved has assumed much greater importance than the character of the powers which the legislature is forbidden to grant by such special act. The decisions do not reveal any very definite conclusion as to what are corporate or municipal or internal, as distinguished from governmental affairs, and the judges have been wont to apply the prohibition of special legislation, without discrimination, to all matters actually attended to by the territorial divisions or their officers. Thus, in the case of Horton *v.* Mobile School Commissioners,[1] it was decided that an act repealing all laws "except those enacted for municipal purposes upon the subject of taxation," did not repeal the laws incorporating and establishing the Mobile School Board. Judge Peters, in rendering the opinion of the court, says : " The word 'municipal' in this exception has no well-defined technical meaning, nor does the language of the revenue act seem to confine its import to any very narrow bounds. It is evidently used in a general, and not in a particular, sense, . . . applicable to incorporated bodies organized for the accomplishment of great and important public purposes, which, for the sake of unity and successful admin-

[1] 43 Alabama, 598.

istration, needed a body corporate and special laws for its management." This failure to discriminate has resulted in an unduly wide interpretation of the term "corporate, municipal, or internal affairs," which is made to include many matters that, in other branches of the law, are regarded as public and governmental in character. Thus, in the case of Commonwealth *v.* Patton,[1] already referred to, it was held that a special act affecting the system of judicial administration came within the constitutional prohibition of special acts relating to the affairs of counties and towns. In the same way it has been held that acts special in character, relating to township roads and the police force, were, under a similar restriction, unconstitutional.[2] In most other branches of the law all these matters — the administration of justice, of highways, and of the police — are regarded as matters rather of central than of local concern. On the other hand, it has been held that, notwithstanding the existence of a constitutional provision, forbidding the legislature to incorporate cities, towns, and villages, by special act, the legislature may, by such an act, provide for the incorporation of a sanitary district,

---

[1] 88 Penn. St. 258.

[2] State *v.* Township Committee of Northampton, 14 Atlantic Reporter, 587; Board of Chosen Freeholders *v.* Buck, 51 N. J. Law, 155; Clark *v.* Cape May, 14 Atlantic Reporter, 581.

with powers of taxation, which has no regard for existing boundaries of previously created municipalities. Such a construction enables the legislature practically to take out of the control of the districts which have been incorporated prior to the passage of the constitution the management of all those matters which may be put under the rather vague term "sanitary affairs," many of which are somewhat local in character. This opens the way for an almost complete nullification of the constitutional provisions.[1]

The only court which seems to have clearly seized the distinction between corporate and governmental powers would seem to be that of Ohio. In this state the conferring of corporate powers by special act is not permitted by the constitution. But the court has held that it was perfectly proper for the legislature by special act to provide for the appointment of a board of police commissioners in a city, on the ground that the board of commissioners upon whom the powers were conferred was not a corporation, and that, therefore, the statute, though special, was not unconstitutional.[2]

[1] Wilson v. Board of Trustees, decided in Illinois and reported in 27 North-Eastern Reporter, 203. See also People v. Draper, 15 N. Y. 532; Metropolitan Health Board v. Heister, 37 N. Y. 661; People v. Pinckney, 32 N. Y. 397.

[2] State v. Covington, 29 Ohio St. 111, approved in State v. Baughman, 39 Ohio St., 455.

Notwithstanding this general failure to discriminate between municipal and purely governmental affairs, it may perhaps be well to consider the decisions which have held unconstitutional special acts interfering with internal affairs of various districts. In the first place, it has been decided that the legislature may not provide a general system of administrative organization for a particular county. Such an act is held to regulate its internal affairs.[1]

It is improper also, by special act, to extend the boundaries of a particular city.[2] Further, it has been generally held that any attempt of the legislature to regulate the duties or salaries of municipal officers, *i.e.* the officers whose duties are in connection with the public works of the city, is forbidden by any of these constitutional provisions. This is the rule laid down in State *v.* Pugh,[3] where it is held that if the constitution provides

---

[1] Mortland *v.* Christian, 52 N. J. Law, 521, 537.

[2] City of Wyandotte *v.* Wood, 5 Kansas, 603. See also City of Westport *v.* Kansas City, 103 Missouri, 141, where it was held that, when the constitution gives cities power to frame charters for their government consistent with and subject to the constitution and laws of the state, if a charter contains a provision fixing the limits of the city, the legislature may not, by special act, change those limits. But see State *v.* Warner, 4 Washington, 773, where it was held perfectly proper for the legislature, under such a constitutional provision, to extend the limits of a city, provided that they were not fixed by the charter. [3] 43 Ohio St. 98, 110.

that "the general assembly shall pass no special act conferring corporate powers," the legislature may not pass a special act giving the municipal council of a city the power to appoint a board of control, to which was to be given the power to appoint new officers to be confirmed by the council and to supervise the public works of the city. So also an act regulating the salaries of officers and imposing new duties upon county auditors in all counties of over one hundred thousand and less than one hundred and fifty thousand inhabitants is void, where the constitution forbids the legislature to pass any local or special laws regulating the affairs of counties, cities, and towns.[1] It has been held also that an act special in character giving the mayor and aldermen the power to appoint a city physician is unconstitutional where there is a constitutional provision prohibiting the legislature from regulating by special and local legislation the internal affairs of cities.[2]

A number of cases have arisen in the courts of Illinois on the question as to what are corporate officers and corporate powers. The constitution provided that the legislature should not grant power to levy taxes for corporate purposes to other than corporate officers. In the case of Harward

[1] See McCarthy v. Commonwealth, 110 Penn. St. 243.
[2] State v. Simon, 22 Atlantic Reporter, 120.

v. The St. Clair and Monroe Levee & Drainage Co.,[1] the attempt had been made to give powers of taxation for levee and drainage purposes to a private company, and the court said: "As the object of the constitutional clause was to prevent the legislature from granting the power of local taxation to persons over whom the population to be taxed could exercise no control, it is evident that by the phrase 'corporate authorities' must be understood those municipal officers who are either directly elected by the population or appointed in some mode to which they have given their consent." This case is of value not only in so far as it defines the term "corporate authorities" under the laws of Illinois, but also as it indicates that drainage and sewerage powers are corporate rather than governmental in character. In Illinois it has also been held that the construction and maintenance of parks is to be regarded as a corporate purpose, that officers for the administration of parks are also corporate authorities, and that, therefore, under the constitutional provision giving the power to levy taxes for corporate purposes to corporate authorities, the legislature could not appoint certain persons as park commissioners and give them the power to purchase and construct parks to be paid for by a municipal cor-

[1] 51 Illinois, 130.

poration. Where the legislature had attempted to do this the courts refused a *mandamus* to force the city of Chicago to issue bonds to pay for the parks.[1] A somewhat similar conclusion was reached by the court of Michigan in what is known as the "Detroit Park case."[2] In this case both the facts and the decision were very much the same; and Judge Cooley advanced the view that our system of government is based upon a right in the different localities to govern themselves, and that an attempt by the legislature to construct city parks without the consent of the city would violate this fundamental right, and would, therefore, even in the absence of a specific prohibition, be unconstitutional. The same decision was reached also in the case of People *v.* Hurlbut.[3] Here the legislature had passed an act to establish a board of public works for the city of Detroit, and had named the members of the board in the act. The court held that the act was unconstitutional, not only on the general ground that the privilege of local self-government was a part of the American system, but also because the constitution of Michigan provided that municipal officers should be elected or appointed in such manner as the

---

[1] People *v.* The Mayor, etc., of Chicago, 51 Illinois, 17.
[2] People *v.* The Detroit Common Council, 28 Michigan, 228.
[3] 24 Michigan, 44.

legislature might direct. It was held that this provision, taken together with other provisions of the constitution, assumed that such municipal officers were to be elected or appointed by the people or the authorities of the municipality, and that the legislature had no right to assume control over the appointment of officers who, like commissioners of city works, were purely local in character. In Ohio, however,[1] an act general in character which gave the Governor power to appoint boards of public works in cities was held to be perfectly constitutional; and, in Massachusetts, the view is repudiated that, in the absence of special constitutional provisions, the American system of government is based upon the local self-government idea.[2] Finally, this right of home rule is not recognized even in such states as California, where cities have the right to frame their own charters subject to general laws. Here it has been held that a general law passed subsequent to the charter will supersede the charter. This has been held both as to police courts and as to local assessments.[3]

It has also been held that, under any of the

[1] State v. Smith, 44 Ohio St. 348.
[2] Commonwealth v. Plaisted, 148 Mass. 375.
[3] Thomson v. Ashworth, 73 California, 73; People v. Henshaw, 76 California, 436; Ex parte Ah You, 82 California, 339; Davies v. Los Angeles, 86 California, 37.

constitutional restrictions under consideration, it is improper for the legislature by special act to provide for the issue of bonds to build public buildings in counties,[1] for the establishment of a reform school, or for a system of taxation and local assessment.[2] A somewhat similar conclusion has been reached in California. The constitution of California provides: "That it shall be the duty of the legislature to provide for the organization of cities and incorporated villages, and to restrain their powers of taxation and assessment; [and] that each county, town, city, and incorporated village shall make provision for the support of its own officers, subject to such restrictions and regulations as the legislature may prescribe." The court held, on the basis of these provisions and of the general principles of American local self-government, which, it was held, resulted from these provisions and from the constitution as a whole, that the legislature could not order an improvement of a local character to be made in the city and levy an assessment to pay for it.[3] But in the

---

[1] Devine v. Cook County, 84 Illinois, 590; State v. County Court of Jackson County, 89 Missouri, 237.

[2] State v. Philbrick, 15 Atlantic Reporter, 579; Gilmore v. Norton, 10 Kansas, 491, 503; see also Atchison v. Bartholow, 4 Kansas, 124.

[3] See People v. Lynch, 51 California, 15, and Schumacher v. Toberman, 56 California, 508.

absence of these constitutional limitations on the power of the legislature, it may do all of these things, even without the consent of the municipal corporation. Thus it may force a city to expend money, and even incur indebtedness, to erect public buildings,[1] to construct a bridge,[2] and to pay private claims not legally binding.[3]

The question, what is a municipal, as distinguished from a central or state, officer, has also arisen. It must be confessed that the cases upon this point are not very satisfactory; nor are they very numerous, except where police officers are concerned. It has, however, been held in Missouri[4] that the mayor is a municipal officer. In this case, a constitutional provision gave the City Court of Appeals final powers of decision, except in specified cases, among which was the case where the title to office under the state was contested. It was held that the court had final jurisdiction as to a contest relative to the title to the office of mayor, since he was a city and not a state officer. As has been pointed out, the courts of

---

[1] Perkins v. Slack, 86 Penn. St. 382, Philadelphia City Hall Case.
[2] Philadelphia v. Field, 58 Penn. St. 320; Pumphrey v. Baltimore, 47 Maryland, 145.
[3] Guilford v. Supervisors, 13 N. Y. 143; Mayor, etc., of New York v. Tenth National Bank, 111 N. Y. 446; Brewster v. Syracuse, 19 N. Y. 116.
[4] Britton v. Streber, 62 Missouri, 370.

Illinois or Michigan have held also that drainage, levee, and park officers, and officers for municipal public works, are municipal or corporate officers.[1]

As to police officers, the decisions are conflicting. The courts of Michigan, Massachusetts, Nebraska, Kansas, and Maryland hold that they are state and not local officers.[2] On the other hand, the courts of Kentucky and New York hold that police officers are local and municipal officers.[3] In the Kentucky case it was held that, where a constitutional provision required that city officers shall be elected, the legislature may not pass a statute which provides for the appointment of police officers by the Governor. In the New York case it was held that under a constitutional provision which required that city officers shall be elected by the people of the city, or appointed by the municipal authorities thereof, in such manner as the legislature shall direct, the legislature may not make out of the district of the city a police district,[4] and provide that the police commissioner of

---

[1] *Supra*, p. 82-84.

[2] People v. Mahaney, 13 Michigan, 481; Commonwealth v. Plaisted, 148 Mass. 374; State v. Leavey, 22 Nebraska, 474; State v. Hunter, 38 Kansas, 578; and People v. Mayor, 15 Maryland, 376.

[3] Shad v. Crawford, 3 Metcalfe, Kentucky, 207; People v. Albertson, 55 N. Y. 50; Evansville v. The State, 118 Indiana, 426; State v. Denny, 118 Indiana, 382.

[4] In this case, the legislature had attempted to transform the city of Troy into the Rensselaer police district.

such district should be appointed by the Governor and the Senate, inasmuch as the constitution intended to insure to the well-recognized localities, such as the cities, the management of their own local affairs, among which is to be included the care of the police. It is only fair to the courts of New York to say that where the attempt was made by the legislature to form several existing municipal corporations into large districts, for the purpose of the management of the police in its various branches, such as the preservation of the peace and the care of the public health and safety, they held that the constitutional provision did not apply which assured to cities the right to elect their own officers, and did not prevent the legislature from providing for the appointment by the Governor of the officers placed at the head of these districts.[1] In the case of Astor v. The Mayor,[2] the court went still further, and held that the legislature might confer local assessment powers, which had theretofore been exercised by the common council, upon commissioners of parks, who had previously thereto been appointed by the Governor and the Senate. This would seem to indicate that the legislature might take the manage-

---

[1] People v. Draper, 15 N. Y. 532; Metropolitan Health Board v. Heister, 37 N. Y. 661; People v. Pinckney, 32 N. Y. 397.
[2] 66 N. Y. 567.

ment of the city parks, also, into its own control. In the Indiana cases, already cited, somewhat the same view was adopted as was adopted in the case of People *v.* Albertson, and it was held that police and fire officers could not be appointed by the legislature, nor could officers who had to do with the management of city streets. In the Indiana cases, however, it must be noticed that the act of the legislature provided for the appointment of such officers by the legislature itself, and that, while the court holds that such legislation violates the fundamental rights of local self-government which under the theory of American government are guaranteed to the various local corporations, still the constitution was interpreted as preventing the legislature from exercising any executive powers; and it was felt by the court that appointment was an executive act, and that therefore the power of appointment could not be exercised by the legislature, although it was admitted that the legislature might regulate the method in which the power of appointment might be exercised by a distinctively executive authority.[1]

This consideration of the decisions of the courts in construction of the constitutional provisions adopted in order to insure municipal corpora-

[1] See also State *v.* Covington, 29 Ohio St. 111, already cited, *supra* p. 80.

tions a greater freedom from legislative interference, cannot fail to impress us with the feeling that these provisions have not fulfilled the expectations of those who advocated their passage. It is true, indeed, that the courts, in their interpretation of these provisions, have given a very wide meaning to the term "municipal," or local or internal affairs, including within it matters which, in other branches of the law, are regarded as governmental and not corporate in character, as affecting the state as a whole, rather than a locality. But the term "special act" has been so narrowly defined as actually to permit the legislature, at almost any time that it may see fit, so to frame a law that it would apply to only one of the cities within the state, and yet be perfectly constitutional. The distinction which the courts make between an act which has merely temporary application, and which, if special, will be unconstitutional, and an act which is passed for all time, which may thus bring within its provisions all cities of a class, and which is therefore general and constitutional, even if it affects at the time of its passage only one city, may be logical, but it certainly renders the constitutional provisions almost futile, from the point of view of securing to municipal corporations immunity from special legislative action. The very narrow meaning given to the term "special act" and the resulting possibility of much legislation which is very special in character, notwithstanding the existence of constitutional provisions attempting to prohibit it, have led some of the states, particularly those which have recently adopted their constitutions, to limit still further the power of the legislature over municipal corporations. This is done by fixing in the constitution the maximum number of classes into which municipal corporations may be divided by the general municipal corporations acts. The number usually determined upon is four. This is the case in Colorado,[1] Missouri,[2] South Dakota,[3] and Wyoming.[4] Two of the constitutions go even further, not only providing the maximum number of classes, but also fixing the population which will cause cities to be included within the classes thus provided. These are Kentucky, which provides six classes,[5] and New York, which provides three classes.[6]

We can hardly blame the courts, however, for their interpretation of these constitutional provisions. For we must admit that classification of cities must be permitted under such provisions. As Judge Paxson points out,[7] if the classification

---

[1] Constitution, XIV., Sec. 13.
[2] Constitution, IX., Sec. 7.
[3] Constitution, X., Sec. 1.
[4] Constitution, XIII., Sec. 1.
[5] Constitution, Sec. 156.
[6] Constitution, XII., Sec. 2.
[7] Wheeler v. Philadelphia, 77 Penn. St. 338.

of cities is not regarded as constitutional, certain cities will be deprived of all means of development. But when we once admit that classification of cities is proper, the logical result must be that which the courts have reached. The truth is, this device for insuring to municipal corporations that power to govern themselves, which is everywhere regarded as extremely necessary, is not elastic enough under our system of enumeration of and strict construction of municipal powers. No general law can, if it has to descend into details, be sufficiently comprehensive to apply with advantage to all the cities within its jurisdiction. It is not possible in a state where the geographical conditions vary widely in different parts, to pass a general law which, even at any given time, will permit all the cities to make the best use of their powers. When we consider the changes of economic and social conditions under our present rapidly advancing civilization, we must recognize even more clearly the impossibility of framing any general law, which descends at all into details, for application to the future as well as to the present. Indeed it is worthy of note that of the four states which fix the number of classes of cities at four, only one, viz., Missouri, has attained any important municipal development; and the law of this state permits local development through the power given the larger cities to formulate their own charters. In New York, which fixes the number of classes at three, it is to be noticed, as will be pointed out, that special legislation is not prohibited. On account of the difficulty of fixing by general law the details of heterogeneous municipal organizations, we hear, from time to time, in some of the states which have adopted this method of home rule, a demand that return shall be made to the old method of special charters and special and local legislation. Such a demand was made only a few years ago in New Jersey. When we remember how little effect these constitutional provisions forbidding special legislation have, as a result of the definition of a "special act," we must admit that a demand for a return to the old system of unlimited special legislation is strong evidence of the impracticability of such a system of regulating municipal affairs under the legal conditions which confront us in this country.

These considerations are not, however, the only ones which militate against such methods of regulating municipal affairs. The development of the municipality within the last century in this country as an agent of the state government, makes it absolutely necessary that the central government of the state shall have an important control over the municipality. Were the municipality now what it was in its early history, merely an organization for the satisfaction of local needs, this control would not be so necessary; but under present conditions, its existence and its frequent exercise are indispensable to the proper and uniform administration of many matters which are usually attended to by municipal officers at the present time. The great difficulty which the courts have had in distinguishing municipal from public or governmental affairs makes it extremely hazardous to tie the hands of the legislature, which is in our system the only guardian of uniform administration. If the legislature is deprived of its control, business of really general character may be variously conducted in different parts of the state, with a resulting lack of uniformity, and possible inequalities of the burdens of the people in the different parts of the state, as, *e.g.*, in the case of taxes, or may be attended to inadequately by the officers of some particular municipal corporation, with disastrous effect to the people of the state at large, as, *e.g.*, in the case of the public health. These dangers, it must be conceded, are very largely avoided by the narrow definition which the courts have given to the term "special act"; but it must also be admitted that in avoiding these dangers the courts have, at the same time, almost nullified the constitutional provisions which they were called upon to interpret, and have left the municipality, almost as much as before the adoption of these provisions, at the mercy of the legislature. This is true even under the Missouri method, which has been adopted also in California and Washington. For here general laws may modify charters adopted by particular cities, and general laws may be very special in their application.

Thus, from whatever point of view we regard the matter, we are forced to the conclusion that these methods of providing for municipal home rule are not proper for the United States. It was this conclusion which undoubtedly forced the recent constitutional convention of the state of New York to abandon them all and to incorporate into the new constitution of the state, which was adopted last November, a provision which, in its entirety,[1] is quite novel in American constitutional law, — a provision which, it was hoped, was framed in such a way as both to avoid the possibility of its complete nullification by the courts through their power of interpretation, and also to afford an elastic and adaptable method of regulating the

---

[1] Several of the earlier state constitutions have provided for a public hearing in regard to local acts. See, e.g., Arkansas, Art. V., Sec. 26; Missouri, Art. IV, Sec. 54; New Jersey, Art. IV., Sec. 7, p. 9.

relations of the legislature to municipal corporations.

The new constitution of New York[1] specifically defines special acts relative to cities. It says that all cities shall be classified according to population, the first class including all those having a population of 250,000 or more, the second class, all having a population of 50,000 and less than 250,000, and the third class embracing all other cities. It goes on then to say: "Laws relating to the property, affairs, or government of cities and the several departments thereof, are divided into general and special city laws. General city laws are those that relate to all the cities of one or more classes. Special city laws are those which relate to a single city or to less than all the cities of a class." But the constitution does not take the further and dangerous step of prohibiting special legislation. It provides merely that a copy of every city bill shall be immediately transmitted to the mayor of the city affected by it, and that either the mayor or the mayor and council of the city concurrently shall, after a public hearing, signify either their approval or disapproval of the particular bill. In case of disapproval the bill may not become a law until it has been re-enacted by the legislature; and in all cases it is subject, like other

[1] Article XII., Sec. 2.

bills, to the action of the Governor. The constitution further provides that the bill must be acted upon by any city affected by it within fifteen days after receipt of a copy thereof by the city officials, and failure of a city to take action is to be regarded as a disapproval of the bill. Finally it is provided that in all cases special city laws shall, after they have been finally passed, have added to their title, "accepted by the city," or "passed without the acceptance of the city," as the case may be.

While this method of limiting the power of the legislature over cities does not, of course, ensure to the cities an absolute immunity from legislative control over purely local matters, it corrects the most serious evil of the old system of special and local legislation. This was that many city bills were rushed through the legislature without the knowledge of the officers of the city or without the knowledge of the people of the city who might be affected by the laws. Now, however, the constitution specifically requires the legislature to provide for a public notice and opportunity for a public hearing concerning any such bill in every city to which it relates.

CHAPTER VI

THE MEANS OF DELIMITING THE SPHERE OF PRIVATE ACTION OF MUNICIPAL CORPORATIONS IN THE AMERICAN LAW

It may, at first sight, seem remarkable that this interference on the part of the legislature in local affairs, which the courts seem to have been unable to prevent, should have occurred in a country, one of whose most fundamental and historic principles has always been supposed to be local self-government. But it must be remembered that the English idea of local self-government, which was later adopted here, was never based on any clear-cut distinction of central from local business. The local areas were, with the exception of the boroughs which began to be incorporated about the end of the fifteenth century, not considered corporations (the county was not incorporated in England until 1888) with business of their own to perform, but mere administrative circumscriptions, in which general state business was to be attended to.[1] The idea of local corporate autonomy was very unclear, if it was held at all.

In the United States we have further decentralized the English system by the very general introduction of the elective principle for local officers, who are generally free from all central administrative control. A natural result of this decentralization has been the increase of the power of the legislature over the actions of local bodies; for the legislature has become the only body in the state having the power to insist upon the uniformity in administrative methods, which, in some branches, is so essential. This legislative interference is therefore perfectly natural, notwithstanding the principle of local self-government (which might better be termed local self-administration), which has always been supposed to be at the basis of our governmental system. In addition to thus decentralizing the original English administrative system, we have also incorporated our local areas,[2] after continental examples

---

[1] Russell v. Men of Devon, 2 T. R. 672; Ward v. County of Hartford, 12 Connecticut, 406.

[2] In Massachusetts the towns were incorporated in 1785. 9 Gray, Mass. 511, note. In New York both the town and the county were fully incorporated in 1829. N. Y. Revised Statutes of 1829. The chapter devoted to the towns is explained by the original reports of the revisers to the legislature in 1827, in which it is said that "this article is wholly new in its present form." It is added that such an

which had at quite an early time been followed in England in the incorporation of the borough.[1] The purpose of incorporating these local areas was to make them subjects of the private law, so that they might own property and sue and be sued.[2] The effect, however, of incorporating them was also to protect them as persons, subjects of the private law, against the legislature, and to recognize that they might act in a *quasi*-private capacity, as well as in a governmental capacity. The first effect of the incorporation of the local areas is seen in the fact that they may own property of which they may not be deprived by legislative action any more than any other corporation or private individual.

important matter as the corporate capacity of these areas should have some firmer legal basis than "judicial legislation." The judicial legislation referred to is to be found in a series of judicial decisions recognizing the corporate character of towns which had been recently made, and which had been without doubt influenced by the corporate character of the old Dutch towns, due to general continental administrative ideas. See North Hempstead *v.* Hempstead, 2 Wendell, N. Y. 109 ; Denton *v.* Jackson, 2 Johnson, Ch. 320, 325.

[1] This idea was taken from the Canon Law.

[2] The inconveniences of the old English system, in accordance with which the localities are not incorporated, may be seen from the cases of Jackson *v.* Hartwell, 8 Johnson, 422 ; Jackson *v.* Cory, *Ibid.* 385; Hornbeck *v.* Westbrook, 9 Johnson, 73 ; and Jackson *v.* Schoonmaker, 2 Johnson, 230, which held that counties and towns could not, because they were not corporations, become grantees of lands or benefit under reservations in deeds.

Thus, from quite an early time, it was recognized that, as a result of the provision of the United States Constitution, which has been reenacted in most of the state constitutions, that no person shall be deprived of property for public purposes, except by due process of law, and upon being paid just compensation therefor, municipal corporations are protected in the property which they own in a purely private capacity, and which is not devoted to public governmental purposes, in much the same way as are ordinary private individuals. Such property is distinguished clearly, by the decisions of the courts, from property held for the purposes of general state government, which is subject to the regulation of the legislature, and is not regarded as protected by the provisions of the constitution relative to the deprivation of property, without the payment of just compensation. This matter is of such importance that its detailed treatment will be deferred to a special chapter.

In the second place, one of the fundamental constitutional restrictions of the taxing power of the legislature is, that the purpose of all taxation must be public.[1] A corollary of this rule is that a tax on the people of a local corporation must, to be valid, be levied for a purpose pertaining to

[1] Loan Association v. Topeka, 20 Wallace, 655.

it.[1] This rule loses much of its usefulness as a means of determining what are purposes pertaining to the locality, owing to the fact that the relation of the purpose of the tax to the locality which is taxed, is governed, very largely, by the benefits which the locality is supposed to receive from the tax, which are, in their turn, largely determined by the legislature.[2] Thus it has been held that the legislature may impose a tax on a town to build a canal, a means of general communication,[3] on a village or town, for part of the expenses necessitated by the erection of a normal school, or an agricultural college,[4] and also for levees.[5] Further, the historic principles of the original English and American system of local self-government gave into the hands of the localities a large part of the work of the central state government. The matters which have been for so long a time attended to by the localities at their own expense, are regarded as interesting, and, therefore, pertaining to, them, although theoretically they may pertain more to general state government.

For these reasons a consideration of the cases

[1] See Burroughs on *Taxation*, pp. 13 *et seq.*
[2] Cooley, *Taxation*, 2d ed., p. 149.
[3] Thomas *v.* Leland, 24 Wendell, 65.
[4] Gordon *v.* Cornes, 47 N. Y. 608; Merrick *v.* Amherst, 12 Allen, Mass., 500–504; Marks *v.* Pardue, 37 Indiana, 155.
[5] State *v.* Clinton, 26 Louisiana Annual, 561.

decided in interpretation of this fundamental restriction of the taxing power, that the purpose of the tax, in order that it be valid, must pertain to the locality which is taxed, becomes of comparatively little value in aiding us in determining what are local or municipal purposes. At the same time, it cannot be denied that a number of cases refuse to allow the legislature full discretion in this matter, but claim that it may not force a locality to expend money for purposes of interest alone to the state at large. Thus it has been held that the legislature may not force a locality to pay the expense of improving the navigation of a river used for general state commerce,[1] nor to raise money by taxes in order to take stock in a railway company,[2] nor to pay for military bounties.[3] Further, it is held that municipal corporations may not without legislative authorization expend money for either of these purposes,[4] but that both these purposes are of a sufficiently public nature to justify the raising of money therefor by localities, where they have

---

[1] Ryerson v. Utley, 16 Michigan, 269. See also Garrard County Court v. Navigation Company, 10 American Law Register, 151, 155, 158.

[2] People v. Batchelor, 53 N. Y., 128.

[3] State v. Tappan, 29 Wisconsin, 664; 9 American Reports, 622.

[4] Stetson v. Kempton, 13 Mass. 272; 7 American Decisions, 145; Curtis v. Whipple, 24 Wisconsin, 350; Kelly v. Milwaukee, 127 U. S. 139; Concord v. Robinson, 120 U. S. 165.

been specially authorized so to act by the legislature.[1] But of late constitutional provisions have very often recognized that the building of railways, and indeed that the aiding of any private corporations, is not within the proper sphere of municipal action, and have prohibited such action on the part of municipalities. These are the only two instances in which the power of the legislature over municipal corporations and local bodies generally is limited in the original Federal or state constitutions as interpreted by the courts, and owing to the great discretion which is permitted to the legislature in deciding what is a local purpose, they are not of very great value, either in restricting the power of the legislature, or defining a sphere of municipal home rule, except in so far as they do afford a substantial protection to municipal property.

But while, under the original constitutions, the legislature would seem to have almost complete power over municipal corporations, on the ground that they are governmental bodies, in other branches of the law relative to municipal corporations, we find a distinct acknowledgment of their private

---

[1] Booth v. Woodbury, 32 Connecticut, 118; Kinkle v. Franklin, 13 Minnesota, 127; 97 American Decisions, 226; Sparkes v. Mayor, 21 Penn. St. 147; Whiting v. Sheboygan Railway Company, 25 Wisconsin, 167; Olcott v. Supervisors, 16 Wallace, 678.

character, resulting from the fact of their incorporation. It is now distinctly recognized that they may have private legal liabilities, although as organs of government they are usually subjects of the public rather than the private law.

The rule of law with regard to the liability of the government is, that it is irresponsible, except in so far as it has been made responsible by special statutes. This rule is applied to governmental contracts, not because the liability of the government for contracts is not recognized,[1] but because the courts have not, in the absence of special statutes, jurisdiction of suits against the government based on contracts. Inasmuch, however, as the local areas have been incorporated in order that they may be subjects of private law, and may sue and be sued, the rule as to the immunity of government from liability on contract has no application to municipal corporations, which are so liable in almost the same way as individuals and private corporations, even when acting as representatives of the government.

[1] A theoretical liability on the part of the government for contracts is, as a matter of fact, recognized. Thus in a suit by the government against an individual, the individual may oppose a counter-claim, provided such counter-claim is not larger than the demand of the government against him. United States v. McDaniel, 7 Peters, 16; United States v. DeGroot, 5 Wallace, 419; United States v. Eckford, 6 Wallace, 434. See also on the general principle, Langford v. United States, 101 U. S. 341.

In the case of the liability for torts, however, the position of the municipal corporation as an agent of government has an important influence. For, while the government recognizes in theory its liability for contract, it does not recognize any liability for torts.[1] Now, as the municipal corporation is both a corporation which is a subject of the private law, and an agency of the state government, we have two distinct rules of liability for the tortious acts of its agents. When it acts as a corporation, a subject of the private law, — that is, when it acts in its true sphere of municipal activity, — it is to be regarded as liable for tort in very much the same way as are ordinary individuals or private corporations. When, however, it acts as an agent of government, it shares in the immunity of the government for the tortious acts of its agents.

Finally, one of the principles of the law of municipal corporations is that they may, so far as they possess private property, alien such property, without the necessity of special authorization by the legislature, but that in so far as they, as governmental agencies, possess property which is used for the purposes of public governmental adminis-

---

[1] Gibbons v. The United States, 8 Wallace, 269; Langford v. United States, 101 U. S. 341; Clodfelter v. State, 86 N. C. 51; Lewis v. The State, 96 N. Y. 71.

tration, they may not alien it, except they have been specifically authorized so to do by the legislature. This question of alienation may come up, as a result of involuntary alienation, that is, the sale of their property on execution, and the same rule is here applicable, namely, that private property may be sold on execution, while public property, which is held in trust for public governmental purpose, may never be so sold.

It will be seen thus that, notwithstanding the failure of the legislature to delimit a sphere of municipal autonomy in which its interference should not extend, the courts have, in those branches of the law of municipal corporations which do not relate to the control of the legislature over these bodies, been able to distinguish between the local and *quasi*-private and the public and governmental functions of municipal corporations, and have assured their private property rights from legislative invasion. It will be seen also that the application of all these principles of the private law to these governmental bodies, this recognition of the private side of municipal action, rests upon one fundamental private-legal conception, *i.e.* the *quasi*-private corporate nature and capacity of municipal corporations. For as parts of the government and not as *quasi*-private corporations, they may neither own property assured against central legislative control and regulation, nor commit torts. This idea of corporate capacity and liability is, however, foreign to the original English and American law as applied to local bodies. This law was so thoroughly permeated with the Anglo-Norman ideas of governmental centralization as to make it impossible to recognize any autonomous rights or private legal duties as pertaining to the local areas, which were not really legal persons, but merely governmental districts. Thus the duty of parishes to keep highways in repair was enforced not by a private action but by indictment, a public remedy. The influence of the non-corporate idea may still be seen in New England in the rule that the property of each resident in the town is liable to be seized to satisfy a judgment against the town.[1] It is only, therefore, as a result of continental influences that the English and American law has been led to regard the local areas as possessing corporate and *quasi*-private rights and liabilities separate and apart from their public and governmental powers and duties. This rule of law, which has always obtained on the continent, originated in the feudal system which had greater influence in continental Europe than in insular England. One of the fundamental

[1] Bloomfield v. Charter Oak Bank, 121 U. S. 121, 129; Hill v. Boston, 122 Mass. 344, 349.

principles of that system was local autonomy. When joined with the Roman law idea of corporate capacity, it resulted naturally in the recognition of local governmental corporations with a sphere of local action apart from that of the state as a whole.

In the succeeding chapters, the attempt will be made to examine in detail the subjects touched upon in this, to determine what is the sphere of private action of municipal corporations recognized by our law of torts and by the law relative to the constitutional protection and the alienation of municipal property.

CHAPTER VII

WHAT ARE MUNICIPAL AFFAIRS FROM THE POINT OF VIEW OF THE LIABILITY OF MUNICIPAL CORPORATIONS FOR TORTS

JUDGE FOOT[1] says: a municipal corporation "possesses two kinds of powers; one governmental and public and to the extent they are held and exercised is clothed with sovereignty; the other private and to the extent they are held and exercised is a legal individual. The former are given and used for public purposes; the latter for private purposes. While in the exercise of the former the corporation is a municipal government, and while in the exercise of the latter is a corporate legal individual." In so far as a municipal corporation acts in this public, governmental capacity, it is regarded by the courts as a part of the government, and therefore is to be governed by the rules of law which are applicable to the government as a whole, that is the public law. One of the rules

[1] In the case of Lloyd v. The Mayor, etc., of New York, 5 N. Y. 369; 55 American Decisions, 347.

of the public law is that the government as a whole is not responsible for the torts which may have been committed by its officers. This rule of law is sometimes said to have originated in the maxim of the English law that the king can do no wrong. In this country, however, it has been held by the supreme judicial authority, namely, the Supreme Court of the United States, that the maxim has no existence in this country either in reference to the government of the United States, or of the several states or of any of their officers.[1] The rule of law as to the immunity of the government for liability for the torts committed by its officers, is really based upon the fact that the government is not regarded as a subject of private law. As has been well said,[2] "The view that the tort is an act of the government by no means entails the government's liability as a logical conclusion. The rule that a tort creates a liability for damages is a rule of private law; it, therefore, applies to relations of the private law only. The position of the state where it acts in the exercise of sovereign and governmental functions is, however, entirely beyond the sphere of private law, and must be judged by different standards. If the courts were

---

[1] Langford v. United States, 101 U. S. 341.

[2] See Freund on "Private Claims against the State," in the *Political Science Quarterly*, Vol. VIII., p. 648.

called upon to administer abstract justice, they might find ample ground in many cases for decreeing reparation of legal injuries by the state, but applying, as they have to, the principles of the common law, they cannot evolve a liability of the state in its sovereign capacity, for the reason that governmental functions do not create civil causes of action, and that rules of private liability are inadequate to govern cases where no private relations exist." Inasmuch, however, as not only the private but also the public law is based upon principles of justice, it is necessary for us, in order to get a satisfactory foundation for this particular principle of the public law, to go further and to ask why should the public law relieve the government from liability for the wrongful acts of its officers? The reason is to be found in the fact that the government is generally acting as the representative of the sovereign, and that it is extremely difficult to hold the representative of the sovereign responsible for the mistakes and negligences of its officers so far as they are acting in this sovereign capacity. "Assuming the wrongful act to be imputable to the state, incident to the unavoidable imperfections of a machinery so complicated as its system of administration, the state enjoys, of course, by virtue of its sovereignty, the privilege of exempting itself from liability. A government which should hold itself responsible to all its citizens for any legal injury suffered by them through the exercise of public powers, which, in other words, should guarantee the just and perfect operation of its administrative and judicial machinery, might find itself confronted with claims and vexed with suits to such an extent as to be driven to a limitation of its liability."[1]

It does not, however, follow, because when the government is acting as the representative of the sovereign it should be held exempt from liability, that this exemption should be extended to those branches of activity where it is acting more as does an ordinary private individual, and is entering into relations similar to the relations of the private law. "The state . . . in dealing with a citizen, does not always act in the character of a sovereign who commands and compels as a representative of law and authority. It can, by virtue of its corporate capacity, equally well entertain relations of the private law becoming a holder of private rights and treating with individuals on the basis of equality. . . . Now, whenever the government thus stands in the position of a holder of private rights, all arguments in favor of its immunity from tort that are drawn from public policy or from

---

[1] *Ibid.* Cf. also the remarks of Judge Walker in Wilcox *v.* Chicago, 107 Illinois, 334, quoted in full, *infra*, p. 138.

the nature of governmental functions, fall to the ground. In such a relation its sovereignty need in no wise be involved, is indeed a mere accident. The obligations incident to the holding of property and the carrying on of industries are imposed by the conditions of social existence, and are essential to the proper functions of ownership. The justification of any exemption from these obligations must be found, not in the privileged position of the owner, but in the exceptional nature of the purposes for which the property is used. Granting that the state can hold property for purposes similar to those of an individual owner, it follows logically that it should hold, on similar conditions. A privilege which cannot be explained by the public functions and powers of the state is anomalous. The principal torts which may be imputable to the government in connection with its private relations are negligence, non-compliance with statutory regulations, nuisance, trespass, and a disturbance of natural easements. It is characteristic of these torts that they violate obligations which are imposed by law upon the ownership or occupation or control of property, that they are sometimes not directly attributable to a specific act of any particular agent, and that the existence of the wrongful condition is usually of some benefit to the owner. The liability of the state in these cases is demanded not only by justice but by the logic of the law. Its immunity cannot be placed upon any convincing argument. It is to be regretted that the courts have always denied the liability of the sovereign in sweeping terms. . . . The law of Germany and France protects the administration from interference by the courts to an extent unknown to our law, yet it is well settled that the state, by entering into private relations, subjects itself to the jurisdiction of the civil courts, and becomes liable like any other holder of private rights. The discussion in Germany as to whether it should be held liable on tort has turned only on the general question whether a corporation can become liable for the torts of its agents; the immunity has never been asserted on other grounds, and a responsibility committed in connection with purely private relation appears now to be the accepted law in both countries."[1] The discussion in France, it may be added, has turned simply on the question which of the courts, the administrative or judicial courts, shall have jurisdiction. This question has been decided in favour of the jurisdiction of the administrative courts.[2] In both England and the United States,

---

[1] Freund, *loc. cit.*

[2] Ducrocq, *Traité du Droit Administratif*, 2d ed., Sec. 1055 *et seq.*

however, the sovereign character of the government has not been lost sight of even when it enters into these private relations, and its immunity from all liability for tort is recognized. This decision has been reached notwithstanding that from the point of view of public policy there can be no objection to recognizing such a liability. The fact that considerations of public policy do not require the adoption of this rule of law is seen even more clearly when we consider the rules of law as to the liability of municipal corporations. So far as they enter into private relations they are regarded, as has been pointed out, as mere "corporate legal individuals," and are therefore held responsible in the same manner as is an ordinary private corporation or individual, and their governmental and sovereign capacity is lost sight of. It has been easy to adopt this view in their case since their corporate capacity has been conferred upon them, not only for their own advantage, but also for the advantage of those who come into dealings with them. The question of their liability has not been obscured by any idea of sovereignty, as it may have been obscured in the case of the government itself.

A somewhat detailed consideration of the rules of law as to the liability of municipal corporations for torts will therefore be of interest, not only from the point of view of the immediate purpose of this work, that is the delimitation of the sphere of private or local action of municipal corporations, but also from the point of view of the general question of the liability of government. For just as we have seen the government gradually being held to a stricter accountability for its contractual acts, so we may expect in the future to see it held also liable for certain of its tortious acts; and what has already been decided with regard to the tortious acts of municipal corporations, will undoubtedly serve as a guide for future decision as to the liability of the government for tort.

Adopting the canon of distinction already alluded to, namely, that a municipal corporation is liable for torts, in so far as it is exercising private and local powers, and is not liable in the case that it is exercising public and governmental powers, let us now ascertain what powers are public and governmental, and what are private and local.

In the first place, it may be laid down as a general principle, that a municipal corporation is not liable for the non-exercise of the legislative power which may have been conferred upon it by the state; nor is it liable for failure to enforce any ordinances that it may have adopted as a result of the exercise of that power. Thus, in the case of

McDade *v.* Chester City,[1] the city of Chester had been given by the legislature the power to pass ordinances, prohibiting the carrying on of any trade or business which might be noxious to the inhabitants, and also the exposure or manufacture or sale of fireworks, or other inflammable or dangerous articles. The plaintiff in the case was injured by the explosion of a manufactory of fireworks, which the city had not suppressed, and which the plaintiff claimed it was its duty to suppress. The court, however, held that this was a governmental matter which had been placed by the legislature in the discretion of the council of the corporation, and therefore refused to hold the city responsible.

Another good case on this general principle is that of Kiley *v.* The City of Kansas.[2] In this case the plaintiff sued the defendant for loss suffered by the death of her daughter, a child fourteen years of age, occasioned by the falling of the brick walls of a burned building, which stood upon private property. The evidence showed that the northern portion of the wall had been left standing two or three months after the fire, and was so unstable as to be dangerous to persons occupying a small house situated some ten feet to the

---

[1] 117 Penn. St. 414; 2 American State Reports, 681.
[2] 87 Missouri, 103; 56 American Reports, 443.

north. At the time of the accident the little girl was visiting the occupants of the house, and the walls fell upon the house, crushing it, and killing her. The defendant had ample notice of the condition of the walls before the accident, and also had power under its charter, by ordinance, to define what should be a nuisance, and to prevent, abate, and remove nuisances, and punish the authors thereof. The court said, "If the defendant is liable at all, it is for a failure to put in force and execution its charter powers relating to either streets or the abatement of nuisances." As a matter of fact, the city had passed an ordinance prohibiting nuisances, which included within its definitions structures like the walls in question, which were regarded as a nuisance. The court further said in deciding the case: "The ordinance in question does not partake of the nature of a contract, but it is a part of the laws passed for the good government of the inhabitants of the city. The city is no more liable for its non-execution, than would be the county if the ordinance were a state statute, and its enforcement left to the county officers and inhabitants."

A similar case is that of Rivers v. The City Council of Augusta,[1] where a child walking upon the streets of a city was set upon and gored by a

[1] 65 Georgia, 376; 38 American Reports, 787.

cow. It appeared that in 1878, cattle were forbidden by ordinance the use of the streets within certain named districts in the city, but that this ordinance was afterwards suspended indefinitely. The court said, in deciding that the city was not liable: "The powers and duties of the City Council of Augusta, under its charter, consist in acts which are legislative or judicial in their nature, and those which are purely municipal. For a failure to perform the first, or for errors of judgment committed in their performance, the corporation is not responsible, because they are deemed to be but the exercise of a part of the state's power, and therefore under the same immunity. . . . The adoption of an ordinance in reference to allowing cattle to run at large in the city, is one which is wholly legislative, and therefore discretionary. It is not liable for neglecting, omitting or refusing to notice the subject, or having noticed it and adopted an ordinance concerning it, then to repeal or suspend [sic] it indefinitely."

In Hill *v.* Charlotte[1] a municipal corporation having power under its charter to make ordinances for the safety of property in the city suspended for a short time the operation of an ordinance forbidding the use of fireworks within the city. During

[1] 72 N. C. 55; 21 American Reports, 451.

such time plaintiff's building was set on fire and destroyed by fireworks used by boys. The court held that the corporation was not liable for the damages thus caused by the suspension of its ordinance, and said in the course of its opinion: "We conceive that nothing can be clearer than that when a general authority is given to a municipal corporation to be exercised through its proper legislative officers to make ordinances for the good government, health, and safety of the inhabitants and their property, it is thereby left entirely to the discretion of these authorities to determine what ordinances are proper for those purposes. Such a charter . . . does not impose such distinct and specific duties as to enable a court to say in any given case that they have not been performed. If a court should undertake to say that by reason of this general grant of power it was the duty of the municipal authorities of Charlotte to pass and retain in force an ordinance prohibiting the use of firecrackers, etc., and that the city was liable to any person damaged by reason of such omissions, there is no reason why the court should not adjudge the city liable in every case where the authorities had omitted to pass any other ordinance which in the opinion of the court would have been proper for the good government of the city, or the health or safety of the inhabitants or of their property.

A court assuming to do this would arrogate to itself the legislative power of the city authorities, and it cannot be supposed possible that any court will be guilty of such an usurpation."

Another good case on this point is that of Forsyth v. Atlanta.[1] In this case the corporation of Atlanta had by ordinance defined the fire limits of the city within which the erection of wooden buildings was prohibited. While the ordinance was in force the city council authorized an individual to erect a wooden building within the said limits, which, taking fire, caused the destruction of plaintiff's building. It was held that the corporation of Atlanta was not responsible for not enforcing or dispensing from its ordinance defining the fire limits.

The only exception to this general rule that a municipal corporation is not liable for the non-exercise of its legislative power, or for the failure to enforce its ordinances, is to be found in the case that it positively licenses something upon the streets of the city which constitutes a nuisance and which seriously interferes with the proper use of the streets as means of communication. The strongest cases upon this point have been decided by the Court of Appeals of the state of New York. In the case of Cohen v. New York[2] the city of

---

[1] 45 Georgia, 152; 12 American Reports, 556.
[2] 113 N. Y. 532; 10 American State Reports, 506.

New York had given a license to an individual, permitting him to keep wagons upon the highway. The thills of the wagon in question were tied up by a string. An individual passing under them was injured by their falling upon him as the result of a collision of the wagon with an ice wagon that was passing in the street. The individual injured subsequently died. An action for damages was brought by his administrators against the city. The court held that the granting of a license, even though such license was justified by an ordinance of the city, and the receiving of compensation for the license for the use of the street for the purpose of storing wagons, was really a maintenance by the city of a nuisance, and that the city could not make use of its legislative powers thus to maintain a nuisance upon the streets. It therefore held the city responsible. In the very recent case of Speir v. The City of Brooklyn [1] the doctrine laid down in the Cohen case was followed. Here the mayor of the city of Brooklyn had granted a license to certain private individuals to give an exhibition of fireworks at the intersection of two crowded and well-built-up streets in the city. A municipal ordinance upon the subject forbade the discharge of any cannon or gun, or the explosion of any fireworks, unless authorized by permit from the mayor

[1] 139 N. Y. 6; 36 American State Reports, 664.

to exhibit the same for public amusement. This ordinance had been usually understood as authorizing the granting of permits for the exhibition of fireworks. The fireworks which were fired off here were very powerful, and one of them, a rocket, set fire to a house fronting upon one of the streets. The Court of Appeals held the city responsible on the ground that it really authorized the discharge of the fireworks, and that the power to pass ordinances and to regulate the use of fireworks did not embrace the power to authorize or legalize nuisances upon the public streets.

A somewhat similar decision was reached in the case of Stanley v. The City of Davenport.[1] In this case the city had, contrary to law, permitted a corporation to use steam motors upon the streets for the purposes of experimentation. An individual using the streets received personal injury caused through his horses being frightened by the steam motor, and the city was held responsible for the damages on the ground that it was negligent in the performance of its duties with regard to the streets. The fact that it had in the exercise of its legislative powers permitted the use of a steam motor upon its streets was not allowed to relieve it from liability.

Another good case is that of McCoull v. The

---

[1] 54 Iowa, 463; 37 American Reports, 216.

City of Manchester.[1] Here the charter imposed upon the city the duty to keep its streets and highways in good and proper condition. It was provided by ordinance that persons building or excavating on lots adjoining the streets might deposit materials in that part of the street opposite their premises not more than one-half of the width of the street, and might be given a special license authorizing the deposit of materials over more than one-half. A person riding in the street at night was injured by falling over a pile of sand left on the street, but not occupying more than half of the width. The city was held liable, and the court, in giving its opinion, laid down a general rule for liability, which is, perhaps, rather more satisfactory than the ground of liability stated in the other cases which have been referred to. It said that the city might not abrogate nor dispense by ordinance with the duties and liabilities imposed by the charter. That "reason and public policy supports the law in holding the city responsible for the negligence or omission of due diligence in the discharge of their charter duties." There is one case which apparently holds that a city is not liable in these cases. This is Burford v. Grand Rapids.[2] Here a city had designated

---

[1] 85 Virginia, 579.
[2] 53 Michigan, 98; 51 American Reports, 105.

a particular street for coasting, and an individual making use of the street was injured by being run into by a sled used upon said street for the purposes of coasting. The city was held not liable, the reason assigned being, however, that the use of the streets for coasting was not, in accordance with the decisions of the courts, necessarily a nuisance, and that though the decision of the council might have been unwise, still it was within their discretionary and legislative power, and the courts could not interfere to revise their decision upon the subject.

The legislative powers, for the exercise or nonexercise of which the city is not to be held liable, embrace, however, many more powers than the mere power of local legislation or ordinance; embrace, as well, the power to decide those many preliminary questions which ought to be settled before the details of any public work, whether it be of purely local or of general interest, can be arranged. "These are questions which call into force the governmental powers of the corporation. They concern ordinarily the expediency of doing the proposed work and the general manner in which it shall be done, and upon these and similar questions municipal corporations act without responsibility. It is for them to decide in what manner they shall exercise their discretionary and judicial powers, and they incur no liability because of their decision upon these questions. Thus in regard to drains and sewers, it is ordinarily for the corporation to decide when it shall have a system of drains and sewers, how extensive the system shall be, and what amount of money the corporation shall expend upon it. These are questions within the province of the municipality as a governmental agency, and the court cannot review its conclusions in regard to them, and until they are settled and some specific work is decided upon, the legal obligation to exercise care is not brought into life."[1] The case of Carr v. Northern Liberties[2] is a good one on this point. In this case the power had been granted by the legislature to a town to construct sewers and other drainage works, but owing to the non-exercise of that power a certain individual's property was flooded and a suit for damages was brought against the corporation. The court said the question before it was, "Have the citizens of our incorporated towns a legal right to call upon the portion of the people thus incorporated to devise and execute such a system of drainage as would secure all private property against all ordinary and extraordinary flooding by rain or melting snow? A little reflec-

---

[1] Jones, *Negligence of Municipal Corporations*, p. 266.
[2] 35 Penn. St. 324; 78 American Decisions, 342.

tion makes it very easy to answer this question in the negative. . . . It becomes manifest how careful we must be that courts and juries do not encroach upon the functions committed to other public officers. It belongs to the province of town councils to direct the drainage of our towns according to the best of their means and discretion, and we cannot, either directly or indirectly, control them in either."[1]

Some of the cases, particularly the earlier cases which, it must be admitted, have been followed in some of the later ones, endeavour to class under this head of discretionary duties all questions relative to the plan to be adopted for the various public works which may be undertaken, and to hold that if any defect in the plan adopted causes the injury the city is not responsible. Perhaps as good a statement as any of this rule may be found in the case of Johnston *v.* The District of Columbia.[2] Here Mr. Justice Gray says: "The duties of the municipal authorities in adopting a general plan of drainage and determining when and where sewers shall be built, of what size and at what level, are of a *quasi*-judicial nature involving the exercise of deliberate judgment and large discretion, and depending upon considerations affecting

---

[1] See also Stackhouse *v.* Lafayette, 26 Indiana, 17; 89 American Decisions, 450.   [2] 118 U. S. 19.

the public health and general convenience throughout an extended territory; and the exercise of such judgment and discretion in the selection and adoption of the general plan or system of drainage is not subject to revision by a court or jury in a private action for not sufficiently draining a particular lot of land." The courts of Michigan seem to have carried this rule the furthest of any. Thus in the case of Detroit v. Beckman,[1] an individual was killed while traversing one of the streets of the city by driving off the end of a culvert, and overturning into the ditch. The accident took place late in the evening, and it was alleged that the city was negligent in causing so short a culvert to be constructed, and leaving so much of the ditch open and unprotected. The ditch and culvert were not of recent construction, and it was not alleged that there was any negligence whatever in the construction except that which pertained to the plan itself. On this ground the court held that the city was not liable. A similar decision is that of Lansing v. Toolan.[2] In this case, the city, in building a sewer, did not provide a sufficient covering, and the court held that this being a part of the plan and not being negligence in the carrying out of the plan, the city was not to be held liable

---

[1] 34 Michigan, 125; 22 American Reports, 507.
[2] 37 Michigan, 152.

for damages resulting from the insufficient covering.[1]

The injustice which may result from the logical application of this rule is so flagrant that the later cases have attempted to limit it considerably, if not absolutely to depart from it. Thus the courts at the present time very generally hold that where the defect in the plan results in a direct invasion of the rights of third persons, as, for example, where the result of a plan or system of sewerage will be either the direct casting of water or sewage upon the property of private individuals, or where by reason of the insufficiency of the sewer, the water backs up and overflows the property of individuals, the city which has adopted such a plan will be held responsible for the damage caused by the defects therein.

This is the rule, even of the courts of Michigan, which have gone further, perhaps, than any other, in assuming that a municipal corporation is not liable for a defect in its plan of public works. In the case of Ashley v. The City of Port Huron,[2] it is said: "It is very manifest from this reference to authorities that they recognize in municipal cor-

---

[1] See also City of Denver v. Catelli, 4 Colorado, 25; 34 American Reports, 62; Fair v. Philadelphia, 88 Penn. St. 309; 32 American Reports, 455; Van Pelt v. Davenport, 42 Iowa, 308; 20 American Reports, 622.

[2] 35 Michigan, 296; 24 American Reports, 552.

porations no exemption from responsibility where the injury an individual has received is a direct injury accomplished by a corporate act which is in the nature of a trespass upon it. . . . If the corporation send people with picks and spades to cut a street through it [the private property] without first acquiring the right of way, it is liable for a tort. But it is no more liable under such circumstances than it is when it pours upon land a flood of water by a public sewer so constructed that the flooding must be a necessary result. The one is no more unjustifiable, and no more an actionable wrong, than the other. Each is a trespass, and in each instance the city exceeds its lawful jurisdiction." The same decision was reached in Seifert v. The City of Brooklyn,[1] where it was held that, if the necessary result of the plan of sewerage was to cause the water to back up and to flow upon the property of individuals, the city was responsible.[2]

Finally, certain of the cases hold definitely to the rule that a municipal corporation must adopt a plan for public works which is reasonably safe. In the case of Gould v. The City of Topeka,[3] the

---

[1] 101 N. Y. 136; 54 American Reports, 664.
[2] See also Jones, *Negligence of Municipal Corporations*, p. 270, note.
[3] 32 Kansas, 485; 49 American Reports, 496.

court says: "After a careful consideration of this entire question, we have come to the conclusion that where a street, as planned or ordered by the governing board of the city, is so manifestly dangerous that a court upon the facts says, as a matter of law, that it was dangerous and unsafe . . . the city should be held liable." The same rule is applied in the case of Hitchins *v.* Frostburg.[1] In the decision of this case the court says: "Any particular plan that may be adopted must be a reasonable one, and the manner of its execution thence becomes, with respect to the right of the citizens, a mere ministerial duty."

In all cases, however, where a city has entered upon the execution of a plan of municipal improvements, it is liable for negligence, both in the execution of such a plan and in the maintenance of the completed improvements in proper and safe condition.[2] This liability practically results from the application of the rule that it is liable for the performance of its duty to keep property under its control in a safe condition. This subject is treated in detail later on.

In the second place, a city is not regarded as acting in its municipal or private capacity in the performance of its police duties. It is therefore

---

[1] 68 Maryland, 100; 6 American State Reports, 422.
[2] See Jones, *op. cit.*, 267.

not responsible for the acts or omissions of policemen. For these officers are officers of the government rather than of the municipal corporation. A good statement of the rule is found in the case of Buttrick v. The City of Lowell.[1] In this case, two police officers of the city of Lowell assaulted, arrested, and imprisoned an individual who was standing peaceably upon the sidewalk, talking with another person, and interrupting no one. The court held the municipality not liable for the damages which were caused by the policemen, and said, "Police officers can in no sense be regarded as agents or servants of the city. Their duties are of a public nature. Their appointment is devolved on cities and towns by the legislature as a convenient mode of exercising a function of government ; but this does not render them liable for their unlawful and negligent acts. The detention and arrest of offenders, the preservation of the public peace, the enforcement of the laws, and other similar powers and duties with which police officers and constables are entrusted are derived from the law, and not from the city or town under which they hold their appointment. For the mode in which they exercise their powers and duties, the city or town cannot be held liable. Nor does it make any difference that the acts

---

[1] 1 Allen, Mass. 172; 79 American Decisions, 721.

complained of were done in an attempt to enforce an ordinance or by-law of the city. The authority to enact by-laws is delegated to the city by the sovereign power, and the exercise of the authority gives to such enactments the same force and effect as if they had been passed directly by the legislature. They are public laws of a local and limited operation, designed to secure good order and to provide for the welfare and comfort of the inhabitants. In their enforcement, therefore, police officers act in their public capacity, and not as agents or servants of the city."

The same rule is true as to the negligence of police officers. Thus in the case of Culver v. Streator[1] it was decided that a city was not liable for damages caused to a person by the negligence of a policeman engaged in killing dogs running at large contrary to a city ordinance. In this case the plaintiff, a woman, was shot and severely injured on the public streets by the policeman. Further, the failure of police officers to put down a mob or riot is no ground for action against the city for damages caused by such a mob or riot.[2]

---

[1] 130 Illinois, 238.

[2] Prather v. Lexington, 13 B. Monroe, 559; 56 American Decisions, 585, see note 589; West Co. of Howe v. Cleveland, 12 Ohio St. 589.

The legislature may, however, impose a liability on cities in such a case.¹ The rule as to the non-liability of cities for the exercise of police powers is applied also in the case of licenses which they may have the power to issue. They are liable neither for negligence in the exercise of the power,² nor for damages caused by their refusal to issue a license which should have been granted.³ The only possible exception to this rule is to be found in the cases already cited,⁴ where a city has made use of its powers to license a nuisance.

Cities are exempt from liability for damages caused not only by police officers engaged in the preservation of the peace, *i.e.* constables, but also by all officers exercising police powers in the wide sense of the words, that is, as a general function of government. Thus the city is not liable for the negligence of officers engaged in the inspection of steam boilers.⁵ In this case an inspector of steam

---

¹ Darlington *v.* Mayor, 31 N. Y. 164.

² Fowler *v.* Alexandria, 3 Peters, 398, where an individual was injured by the negligence of a municipal corporation in not taking a bond as required by law from an auctioneer to whom it had issued a license, and was not allowed to recover damages from the city.

³ Duke *v.* Rome, 20 Georgia, 609. White *v.* Yazoo City, 37 Mississippi, 357.

⁴ *Supra*, p. 123.

⁵ Mead *v.* New Haven, 40 Connecticut, 42.

boilers, in making the inspection, negligently subjected a boiler to unusual, unnecessary, and unreasonable pressure, thereby breaking it. The city was held not liable, although the Board of Steam Inspection which appointed the inspector was created under the charter. The duty was regarded as a public one in which the city had no pecuniary interest, and in the performance of which the city was acting as the agent of the government. Nor is it liable for the negligence of health officers. In the case of Bryant *v.* St. Paul,[1] agents of the board of health left open a vault on private premises, after cleaning it, and the plaintiff fell into it and was injured. The city was held not liable, and the court said, in giving its opinion: " The duties of such [health] officers are not of that class of municipal or corporate duties with which a corporation is charged in consideration of charter privileges, but are police or governmental functions, and could be discharged equally well through agents appointed by the state, though usually associated with and appointed by the municipal body." The same is true of the negligence of the fire department, which is regarded as an agency of the state government, rather than an agent of the city. The city is not liable for damages caused by the negligence of members of the fire department,

[1] 33 Minnesota, 289.

either in not putting out a fire,[1] or committed while going to a fire, and resulting in a collision of a fire engine with a carriage.[2] The statement of the public policy of the rule made in Wilcox v. Chicago is an extremely good one, not only from the point of view of municipal corporations, but also from that of the government in general. "If liable for neglect in this case, the city must be held liable for every neglect of that department and every employee connected with it when acting in the line of duty. It subjects the city to the opinion of witnesses and jurors whether sufficient despatch was used in reaching the fire after the alarm was given, whether the employees had used the requisite skill for its extinguishment, whether a sufficient force had been provided to secure safety, whether the city had provided proper engines and other appliances to answer the demands and hazards of fire in the city ; and many other things might be named which would form the subject of legal controversy. To permit recoveries to be had for all such and other acts would

---

[1] Taintor v. Worcester, 123 Mass. 311, where the building of the plaintiff was burned up owing to the fact that the city had shut off the water from the hydrant in his street. See also Robinson v. The City of Evansville, 87 Indiana, 334; 44 American Reports, 770.

[2] Wilcox v. The City of Chicago, 107 Illinois, 334; 47 American Reports, 434.

virtually render the city an insurer of every person's property within the limits of its jurisdiction. It would assuredly become too burdensome to be borne by the people of any large city where loss by fire is annually counted by the hundreds of thousands if not by the millions."

Finally, the city is not liable for the negligence of officers connected with its poor and hospital service. In the case of Maxmilian v. The Mayor, etc., of New York,[1] an ambulance, driven by an employee of the Commissioners of Charities and Corrections of the city of New York, ran over and killed an individual who was attempting to board a street-car. The negligence of the driver of the ambulance was admitted, and the city still was held not liable. Nor is the city liable for the actions of officers who have the care of criminals.[2] In this case, the plaintiff, an inmate of the workhouse of Boston, confined there for the offence of not supporting his family, was injured while engaged in unloading coal, owing to the negligence of the servants and officers of the institution. The city was held not liable on the ground that its action "in establishing a workhouse was purely for the public service and for the general good, in providing for the care and support of offenders for whose maintenance it was responsible."

[1] 62 N. Y. 160.   [2] Curran v. Boston, 151 Mass. 505.

The only cases in which municipal corporations have been held responsible for the negligence of officers connected with the administration of penal or charitable institutions are based upon the fact that the property of such institutions was left in such a condition as to cause damage; and, as will be shown, municipal corporations are held up to a pretty strict account in the performance of their duty of keeping their property in good condition.[1] Even here, however, the cases are not uniform; some of them holding to the rule that, inasmuch as the municipal corporation is in these cases discharging a governmental or public function, it may not be held responsible, notwithstanding that the negligence which has caused the damage has been in connection with property.[2]

We may sum up our conclusions from the consideration of these cases as follows: A municipal corporation is not regarded as acting as a local organization, but rather as an agent of government, when it exercises legislative power both in the case that it issues and executes ordinances

---

[1] See Edwards v. The Town of Pocahontas, 47 Federal Reporter, 269, and Moffitt v. The City of Asheville, 103 N. C. 237; 14 American State Reports, 810.

[2] See La Clef v. The City of Concordia, 41 Kansas, 323; 13 American State Reports, 285. See also the case of Pfefferle v. The Commissioners, 39 Kansas, 432; Stewart v. The Supervisors, 83 Illinois, 341; 25 American Reports, 397.

and in the case that it decides upon the general plan of public improvements. The only exception to the last statement is that it must, according to the later cases, adopt a reasonably safe plan. It is acting in a public and governmental capacity also in the management of police in the wide sense of the word, that is, as embracing the preservation of the public peace, health, and safety.

The only cases where the city may be regarded as acting in a purely municipal capacity, as becoming a subject of the private law of torts, are where it is managing institutions which have been adopted for the good of the inhabitants of the particular district. Under this head we may embrace most notably the care of wharves, of water and gas-works, and of such institutions as markets and wash-houses. It is also regarded as acting in a local and *quasi*-private capacity in so far as it has the management of sewers and drains and public works generally.[1] In all these cases its liability may be based on one of two grounds, viz., that it is managing property, or that the work which is being attended to by it and in whose management the damage has been done is of local and not general interest. Sometimes the distinction between judicial and ministerial duties has

[1] For cases upon this point, see below.

been advanced, but this is being abandoned in those cases where damage has been caused by a flagrant misuse of discretion, as, *e.g.*, in the case of the adoption of a defective plan of public improvements. But in almost all cases where municipal corporations have been held liable for tort, with the exception of negligence in the care of streets, which will be spoken of later on, the duty whose negligent performance has caused the damage has, as a matter of fact, been performed in connection with municipal property and, as will be pointed out, negligence in the management of property of whatever nature is more and more being regarded as a basis for a liability for damages. By the greater weight of authority municipal corporations are also held responsible for the management of streets. The position of the courts with regard to streets is so peculiar, however, that little aid will be derived from a consideration of their decisions on this point, in the determination of the question, When is a municipal corporation acting as a local corporation or as an agent of government? By an almost unanimity of decision, the courts hold that municipal corporations have no property in streets which is capable of being protected against the legislature. Thus Judge Emmott says, in People *v.* Kerr:[1] "So far as the

[1] 27 N. Y. 188, 192, 197–200.

existing public rights in these streets are concerned, such as the right of passage over them as common highways, a little reflection will show that the legislature has supreme control over them. When no private interests are involved or invaded, the legislature may close a highway and relinquish altogether its use by the public. It may regulate such use or restrict it to peculiar vehicles or to the use of particular motive power; it may change that kind of use into another, so long as the property continues to be devoted to public use. . . . Whatever may be the quantity or quality of the estate of the city of New York in its streets, that estate is essentially public and not private property, and the city in holding it is the agent and trustee of the public and not a private owner for profit and emolument. . . . Nor can compensation be demanded by this municipal body in which the title to the property thus acquired has been vested. . . . The title thus vested in the city of New York is as directly under the power and control of the legislature for any public purposes as any property held directly by the state, . . . and its application cannot be questioned by the mere agent of the sovereign power of the state. . . . The interest is exclusively *publici juris*, and is in any respect totally unlike property of a private corporation, which is held for its own benefit and used for its private gain and advantage." They hold also that cities may not without legislative authorization grant the right to use the streets for the purposes of transporting gas or water or for railway purposes to any person or corporation.[1] They very generally hold, on the other hand, however, that municipal corporations are liable for negligence in the performance of their duty to care for streets.[2]

Most of the courts which hold municipal corporations proper liable for negligence in the performance of their duty to keep the streets in proper condition, at the same time recognize that *quasi*-municipal corporations, such as towns and counties, are not, in the absence of statute, liable for neglect to repair the highways.[3] The reasons which have been advanced for this distinction are, however, generally unsatisfactory. In some cases they are even fantastic. The most satisfactory one is that which is advanced by Judge Dillon in

---

[1] Dillon, *Law of Municipal Corporations*, 4th ed., pp. 808, 821, 833.

[2] Barnes v. District of Columbia, 91 U. S. 540. There is, however, considerable conflict upon this point. See Hill v. Boston, 122 Mass. 344, 369, where Judge Gray makes a strong plea for the immunity of municipal corporations from liability for the care of the streets, on the ground that in their care of the streets municipal corporations are acting for the public as a whole, and not for any private and local advantage.

[3] See Barnes v. The District of Columbia, 91 U. S. 540, 551.

his work on municipal corporations, where he says that streets in cities "have peculiar and local uses, distinct from state highways,"[1] and that therefore the duty to care for them is local and *quasi* private rather than governmental in character. This is a much more satisfactory reason than the reason most commonly advanced, that inasmuch as the state has granted valuable franchises to a chartered municipality which is not true of *quasi* corporations, there arises an implied obligation upon the part of such a municipality to carry out the duties imposed upon it in its charter, that this obligation is violated when the municipality is negligent in the performance of its duty, and that therefore every individual, being a portion of the public with which this contract was made, may have an action upon it when injured by the negligence of a corporation.

It is also much more satisfactory than the one which is proposed by Mr. Jones in his work on the "Negligence of Municipal Corporations."[2] He says, after commenting upon this obligation or contract theory of liability: "There is, however, another and more far-reaching reason for insisting upon municipal liability for this negligence. And this is because the duty to keep the streets in

[1] See Dillon, *Law of Municipal Corporations*, 4th ed., p. 1291.
[2] P. 111.

repair is a municipal duty in regard to property rights, which rests upon the corporation as an independent member of society, and the rights of others are infringed if their action for damages for its breach is taken from them by the courts." How can we speak of this duty of repairing streets as being one in regard to property rights when the courts unanimously refuse to recognize that municipal corporations have any property rights in the streets? On this ground, further, how can we account for the common-law distinction in respect to liability for streets and highways between municipal corporations and *quasi*-municipal corporations?

In the difference between the uses of streets and highways to which Judge Dillon alludes is to be found the most satisfactory reason of the difference in the liability of those authorities which have charge of these different means of communication. For, as a matter of fact, streets are not the same as highways. Highways are important to the public at large as means of intercommunication between different parts of the state. Streets, on the other hand, are for the most part used by individuals of a particular locality. It is only in so far as they form part of state roads, which is seldom, that they are of general significance at all. As a general thing they serve as means communication not only for purpose of passage on their surface, but also as a means of permitting municipalities to perform those many duties which a great aggregation of inhabitants requires that they shall perform, as, for example, the carrying away underground of sewage and the distribution of water, gas, heat, and electricity. The courts have recognized in another branch of the law that streets do differ from highways in that streets are regarded as being subject to certain urban servitudes which are not recognized in the case of the ordinary rural highways.[1] Inasmuch as streets are thus used for a series of local purposes for which highways are not used, it is only logical to maintain that the care of streets becomes a local duty. Of course, it would be more logical to recognize at the same time that municipal corporations have property rights in the streets, and the power to designate the uses to which they may be put, but up to the present time, at any rate, the courts have not been willing to go so far in their recognition of the *quasi*-private character of municipal corporations, fearing that the recognition of such property rights would result in too

---

[1] Traphagen *v.* Jersey City, 29 New Jersey Equity, 206; Commonwealth *v.* Tenny, 21 Ohio St. 499; Milhau *v.* Sharp, 15 Barbour, N. Y. 193, 210; Bloomfield, etc., Company *v.* Calkins, 62 N. Y. 386; Eels *v.* Telephone Co., 143 N. Y. 133.

great independence of local action, too great immunity from central legislative control. It is, indeed, true that many of the later constitutional provisions do recognize that municipal corporations have certain property rights in their streets in that they prevent the legislature from granting the use of streets and highways to railway companies without first obtaining the consent of the corporations,[1] which, it is held, may be given on conditions, *e.g.*, that the grantee assume a portion of the burden of their maintenance or pay the city something for their use.[2]

Further, in most of the states where the courts do not recognize that *quasi*-municipal corporations are liable for their performance of their duty to care for the highways, it must be admitted that the legislature has made them so liable; and it may be reasonably urged that the ground of this statutory liability is to be found in their right and duty to care for the highways, which may be regarded as in the nature of a duty or right appertaining to property.

While in the present state of the law it may be safer to regard this common-law liability of municipalities, for negligence in the performance of their street duties, as based on the local char-

[1] See, *e.g.*, Const. N. Y., Art. III., Sec. 18, and *supra*, p. 61.
[2] Dillon, *op. cit*, p. 948.

acter of streets, the property theory of liability has at the same time much in its favour. Its adoption not only affords a satisfactory ground for the statutory liability very generally imposed on *quasi*-municipal corporations, for negligence in the performance of highway duties, but will also bring all cases of liability of public corporations for tort under one head, viz., negligence in the management of all property entrusted to their control. This is being fast adopted as the rule by the courts of this country.

CHAPTER VIII

WHAT ARE MUNICIPAL AFFAIRS FROM THE POINT OF VIEW OF THE LIABILITY OF MUNICIPAL CORPORATIONS FOR THEIR MANAGEMENT OF PROPERTY

NOTWITHSTANDING the general rule, which was considered in the last chapter, that municipal corporations are not liable for damages committed in the performance of public or governmental duties, the courts are beginning to hold that, if the damage was caused by an act or omission connected with the management of property under the control of a municipal corporation, even though the property, in the management of which the act or omission causing the damage was committed, is used for public or governmental purpose, the municipal corporation is liable. The reason for this apparent exception to the general rule, as to liability for torts, is that the duty to keep property under the control of the municipal corporation in a safe condition is in all cases considered to be a private, municipal, or corporate duty, distinguishable from the public duty, for the performance of which the property may be held. While this is unquestionably the tendency of the later decisions, it must, at the same time, be admitted that in their earlier decisions many of the courts did not see their way clear to make this distinction, and allowed the purpose for which the property — through whose negligent management the damage was caused — was held, to control, holding that municipal corporations were liable for negligence in the management of property only when the holding of such property was of pecuniary advantage to their inhabitants. The result of the existence of these two rules is a conflict in the decisions which is absolutely irreconcilable.

It may, however, be laid down as a general principle applied by all the courts, that municipal corporations are liable for the management of property under their control, if such property brings in any revenue to the corporation. This rule is adopted even in New England, where the courts very generally adhere to the view that there is no liability for negligence in the management of public property.[1] Thus, in the case of Oliver v. Worcester,[2] an individual was injured

---

[1] Eastman v. Meredith, 36 N. H. 296; Hill v. Boston, 122 Mass. 344.

[2] 102 Mass. 489; 3 American Reports, 485.

by falling into an excavation made near the city hall, and not guarded properly by the corporation. It was shown by the evidence brought forward in the case, that the city hall, in repairing which the excavation had been made, was used by the city principally for governmental purposes, but that a substantial portion of it, both before and after the time of the accident, the city leased and received rent therefor, either from private persons or from the county. The property, in connection with which the negligence was committed, being used by the city not for governmental purposes exclusively, but, in a considerable part, as a source of revenue, the city of Worcester was held liable for the damages which its negligence had caused.

In the application of this principle, it has been held that municipal corporations are responsible for damages caused by negligence in the management of cemeteries, from which they derive an income;[1] of wharves and docks which are under their control;[2] of water works from which they derive a revenue, and for which they are held responsible in about the same manner as are pri-

[1] Toledo *v.* Cone, 41 Ohio St. 149.

[2] Seaman *v.* New York, 80 N. Y. 239; see also Kennedy *v.* New York, 73 N. Y. 365; 29 American Decisions, 169; and the cases collected by Jones, *The Negligence of Municipal Corporations*, p. 71, note 2.

vate water companies;[1] of gas works, in the same manner as a private corporation;[2] of public markets,[3] and, finally, for damages, caused by a defective wringing machine, kept in a public wash-house, which was rented out, the defect resulting from negligence.[4]

When we come to the consideration of the question of the liability of municipal corporations for the management of public property, property from which they derive no revenue, but which they hold for governmental purposes, we find the matter much more difficult of solution, and a great conflict in the decisions. For here the municipal corporation is acting not in a private capacity, but as an agent of government. It is, therefore, in much the same position as the county or the town. The rule of law with regard to the county or the town upon this subject is somewhat more simple, although it must be confessed that it is not absolutely free of difficulty, and that there is some conflict among the decisions. It has, however,

---

[1] Bailey *v.* New York, 3 Hill, 531; see also Brown *v.* Atlanta, 66 Georgia, 71; Murphy *v.* Lowell, 124 Mass. 564.

[2] Keble *v.* Philadelphia, 105 Pa. St. 41; Western Savings Society *v.* Philadelphia, 31 Pa. St. 175.

[3] Suffolk *v.* Parker, 79 Virginia, 660; 52 American Reports, 640; Barron *v.* Detroit, 94 Michigan. 601; 34 American State Reports, 366.

[4] Cowley *v.* Sunderland, 6 H. & N. 565.

been very generally held that counties and towns are not responsible for damages occasioned by defects in purely public buildings resulting from the neglect of the county or the town to make the repairs necessary for their safety. In the case of Kincaid *v.* Hardin,[1] an individual sustained damage by reason of the negligent construction of a courthouse, and by reason of negligence on the part of the county in not lighting an unguarded and dangerous stairway leading to the court-room. The court held that the county was not liable. The ground of its decision, as stated in the opinion, was that the county was a *quasi* corporation, and that *quasi* corporations, "such as counties, towns, school districts and the like, are not liable for damages in actions of this character, because they are involuntary territorial and political divisions of the state created for governmental purposes, and because they give no assent to their creation, whereas municipal corporations proper are either specially chartered or voluntarily organized under general acts of the legislature." The same principle with regard to towns was adopted in the decision of Eastman *v.* Meredith.[2] In this case the town of Meredith had built a town house to be used for holding town meetings and other public

---

[1] 53 Iowa, 430 ; 36 American Reports, 236.
[2] 36 N. H. 284 ; 72 American Decisions, 302.

purposes. Owing to the negligence of those who built the house, the flooring was unsafe, and on the occasion of an annual town meeting gave way, when the plaintiff, an inhabitant and legal voter in attendance on the meeting, received a serious injury. It was decided that the town was not responsible upon the same ground which was at the basis of the decision of Kincaid *v.* Hardin, viz., that the town did not hold its powers by special grant, and that its organization was imposed upon it without its will or consent.[1] In New England, however, where the towns, owing to the fact that the village organization is not often adopted, are frequently allowed by the legislature to assume duties of a more private character, it was felt necessary, from the beginning, somewhat to limit and restrict this absolute immunity from liability resulting from the fact of the involuntary and public character of the corporation. Thus we find in the case of Bigelow *v.* Randolph,[2] which held that a town in Massachusetts was not liable for an injury sustained by a scholar attending the public school and caused by a dangerous excavation in the schoolyard, due to the negligence

---

[1] Some cases hold, however, that even *quasi*-municipal corporations are liable for the maintenance of nuisances on their property. See Haag *v.* Vanderburgh Co., 16 Indiana, 511 ; 25 American Reports, 655, where a county was held liable for damages caused by a small-pox hospital.   [2] 15 Gray, 541.

of the town officers, the following limitation of the rule as to this immunity from liability: "The rule is applied in the case of towns only to the neglect or omission of a town to perform those duties which are imposed upon all towns without their corporate assent, and exclusively for public purposes, and not to the neglect of those obligations which a town incurs when a special duty is imposed on it with its consent, express or implied, or a special authority is conferred on it at its request."

The purpose of this limitation of the rule is evidently to include those cases, where a town has undertaken some service which it has been allowed by statute to undertake, and which is primarily for its own advantage. It does not purpose to make the town liable for duties of a public character, which the statute merely says that it may assume. This is seen from the facts of the case. The town had assumed the duties of a school district, duties from which it derived no pecuniary advantage, and of a public character interesting the state at large. The fact that the town had assumed this duty, and that it had not been obliged by the legislature to perform it, was not allowed by the court to have any influence upon the decision, but the town was held not liable for negligence in the performance of the duty, notwithstanding that it had assumed it voluntarily, and was held not liable because the duty was of a public nature. That the limitation of the exemption from liability made in this case is not based upon the fact of the voluntary assumption of the duty, is well brought out in the case of Tindley v. The City of Salem,[1] where the court says: "In some instances the legislature determines finally the necessity or expediency [of the performance by a corporation of a given duty], and in others it leaves the necessity or expediency to be determined by the towns themselves, but when determined, and when the service has been entered upon, there is no good reason why a liability to a private action should be imposed, when a town voluntarily enters upon such a beneficial work, and withheld when it performs the service under the requirement of an imperative law. To make such a distinction would not have the effect to encourage towns in making liberal provision for the public good. It is well known that many towns in Massachusetts not bound to do so, voluntarily maintain high schools. It is not to be supposed that the legislature have intended to make such towns liable to private action, when towns required to maintain high schools will be exempt. On the other hand, it has been recognized in numerous cases in this state and elsewhere, that the question of the

[1] 137 Mass. 171; 50 American Reports, 289.

liability of towns does not rest upon this distinction."

Following out the line of reasoning adopted in Bigelow v. Randolph, a town in Massachusetts was held liable for damages caused by its neglect in the management of its water works. Owing to such negligence, water had undermined the roadway, and an individual was injured while driving on the road. The court distinctly stated that the liability was the result of the negligence of the town in the management of an institution from which it derived a revenue, therefore from negligence in the performance of a private duty, and was not a result of the negligence of its statutory duty to keep the highways in good repair.[1]

In Maine also, it has been held [2] that a town is liable for damages caused to an individual, by the negligence of the town officers in permitting a ram kept on its poor farm for the purpose of propagating sheep, to run at large. The court said, in rendering its decision: "The power to own and carry on a farm, carries with it the power to stock and manage it for purposes of profit, in a manner comporting with the ordinary management of such property among farmers. This embraces

---

[1] Hand v. Brookline, 126 Mass. 324.
[2] Moulton v. Scarborough, 71 Maine, 267; 36 American Reports 308.

the raising of cattle, horses, swine, and sheep, and for the propagation of sheep, a town may lawfully keep and own a ram. If it does so, it is not done in the performance of a public duty enjoined upon it by law, but as a voluntary corporate act, as a part of its system for the most economical support of its poor. For all matters connected with the management of the farm by its agents and servants, for the proper keeping and restraining of all domestic animals kept upon it, by its authority for purposes of profit, it undoubtedly rests upon the same liability as persons." A somewhat similar, and even stronger, case is Rowland *v.* Kalamazoo Co. Supts. of the Poor,[1] where it was held that, when the county superintendents of the poor were authorized to maintain a poor farm, and to sell and dispose of the proceeds of the labour of the occupants thereof, and had acted negligently in its management, in that persons in their employ had started fires which extended to and injured adjoining property, the county was liable.

It must be confessed, however, that the limitation of the rule as to exemption of liability, introduced in the case of Bigelow *v.* Randolph, has been unduly extended by some of the courts in their attempt to find a basis for a common-law

[1] 49 Michigan, 553.

liability of towns and counties for neglect in the maintenance of highways and bridges, and property generally. Thus, in the case of Kincaid *v.* Hardin, to which reference has already been made, and which held a county not liable for damages caused by its negligence connected with public buildings, the judge distinguishes the case at bar from the cases where counties had been held liable for negligence in connection with bridges. He bases his distinction on the principle of liability applied to *quasi*-municipal corporations, in the case of Bigelow *v.* Randolph, and conceives that the test of liability applied in that case is to be found in the voluntary assumption of the duty by the corporation. He says: "The respective counties are not absolutely required, by this provision of the statute, to build any particular bridge or to build any bridge whatever. It is a question to be determined by the Board of Supervisors, taking into account the wants and convenience of the public. Now, when they elect to build a bridge, it may very properly be said that under the rule last above referred to [that is, the rule in Bigelow *v.* Randolph] the county incurs a duty by its consent, and should be liable for the negligent performance of it, or for negligently permitting the bridge built by its express consent to become out of repair." This, however, is, as will be noticed, an unfair extension of the limitation, and is not, in the absence of statute, usually sufficient to account for the liability of towns and counties for negligence in the maintenance of highways and bridges, because in most cases the duty to keep highways and bridges in good condition is not one voluntarily assumed by them, but is imposed by the general highway law.

In another case, that of Hannon *v.* St. Louis County,[1] this limitation of the rule as to exemption of liability was carried still further. The county of St. Louis had assumed the power of building a lunatic asylum, and the assumption of the power was afterwards ratified by the legislature, which had not, however, before it was built, even authorized the county to construct the building. During the process of constructing the building, owing to the negligence of those in charge, an individual was injured, and suit was brought against the county for damages. The court held the county responsible, but did not consider, in its opinion, the question as to whether a *quasi*-municipal corporation differed, in any respect, from a municipal corporation proper, nor did it take into consideration the question as to the liability of a municipal corporation proper for the negligent management of property which it held for a purely public purpose. It

[1] 62 Missouri, 313.

simply assumed that municipal corporations proper were thus liable, and then claimed that the *quasi*-municipal corporation, in this instance the county of St. Louis, was liable because it had assumed a power which it was not obliged to exercise, but was merely permitted by the legislature to exercise. Such an application, however, of the exception to the rule as to the non-liability of *quasi*-municipal corporations, contained in the case of Bigelow *v.* Randolph, was, it must be admitted, absolutely unwarranted, while the general impolicy of the rule that corporations are to be held liable for the performance of duties which they have assumed voluntarily is seen by a consideration of the remarks of Judge Allen in the case of Tindley *v.* The City of Salem, already referred to.

We may conclude, then, as a result of this discussion, that the ground of the non-liability of *quasi*-municipal corporations for the management of their property, which is so commonly, though not universally, recognized, is to be found, not in the fact that they are involuntary corporations, nor in the fact that they are merely *quasi*-municipal corporations, that is, that they have an imperfect corporate liability, because, as we have seen, the courts hold that where they are performing a duty of a private character[1] they may be held

---

[1] *Supra*, p. 155.

responsible for its negligent performance, but must be found in the fact that they are, as a general thing, engaged in the performance of public governmental duties, from the performance of which they do not ordinarily obtain any revenue or any particular private advantage. The only branch of the law where the decisions generally seem to assume that their non-liability results from their *quasi*-corporate character, is to be found in the highway law, but this matter is in such a confused condition at the present time, there being three separate rules of law in the different parts of this country, that nothing can really be predicated from the general insistence upon the common-law non-liability of such bodies. Indeed, the public need of their being made liable has been so great that even in those states where the liability is not recognized by the common law, the legislature has generally, as has been indicated, imposed upon them a statutory liability. The real ground, then, of the non-liability of *quasi*-municipal corporations for the negligent performance of their duties, is to be found in the fact that these duties are generally of a public or governmental character. Let us now see how far this rule of law as to the non-liability of governmental bodies for the performance of governmental duties may be applied to the duty of municipal corporations to keep their public buildings in a state of proper repair.

It must be confessed, although there is a considerable conflict, that in most of the decisions, particularly in the earlier ones, and still more particularly in those of the courts of New England, the public character of these buildings has been allowed to govern. Thus, in the case of Wixon v. Newport,[1] it was held that where a child was injured by being scalded and burned in a school, as a result of the negligence of the city in the care of the heating apparatus, the city was not liable, although it had assumed the maintenance of the school. The court says: "The ground of exemption from liability is not that the duty or service is compulsory, but that it is public, and that a municipal corporation in performing it, is acting for the state or public in a matter in which it has no private or corporate interest, and that therefore, inasmuch as it can only act through its officers or servants, it is entitled to have them while engaged in the performance of the duty or service regarded as the officers or servants of the public, and to be exempt from any private responsibility for them."

A somewhat similar decision was reached in the case of Howard v. Worcester,[2] where, though it was admitted that the city was, through its agents,

[1] 13 R. I. 454.   [2] 153 Mass. 426.

negligent in the building of a school-house, whereby a horse was frightened (by negligent blasting), the city was held not liable, because "the building was erected . . . solely for the public use, and with a sole view to the general benefit."

Similar decisions were reached by the Court of Appeals of New York in the cases of Ham v. The Mayor,[1] and in Donovan v. The Board of Education.[2] In both these cases, individuals were injured by the negligent management of school property; and the city, in both cases, was held not liable. In the first case, the reason assigned was that, although "the department of public instruction was formally constituted a department of the municipal government, the duties which it had been required to discharge were not local or corporate, but related and belonged to an important branch of an administrative department of the state"; and that "although the commissioners were appointed by the mayor, they were vested with full power and authority to manage and control the educational institutions of the entire municipality, and to appoint all subordinate officers and employees . . . who were their servants and subordinates." In the latter case, namely, that of Donovan v. The Board of Education of the City of New York, the result reached was the same; but

[1] 70 N. Y. 459.   [2] 85 N. Y. 117.

much greater insistence was laid upon the fact that, by the statute, the care of the educational interests of the city was vested in a board which was, to a certain extent, independent of the city. This independence of the department of public instruction, in the one case, and the board of education in the other, of the ordinary municipal and corporate authorities, would seem to be the controlling factor in the case, inasmuch, as will be shown further on, the courts of the state of New York very generally recognize that municipal corporations are liable for the management of property, even though such property is used in the discharge of a public or governmental duty.

In a late case in Massachusetts, Benton v. The Trustees of the Boston City Hospital,[1] the fact that the city was discharging a public duty in the management of a hospital was held to relieve it from liability to one who, while perfectly properly visiting the hospital to see a grandchild who was being treated therein, and for whom she was paying money, was injured, owing to the negligence of the superintendent of the hospital.

Such are some of the decisions applying this principle,—that municipal corporations are not liable for negligence in the discharge of public duties—to the duty of managing property used for

[1] 140 Mass. 113.

a public purpose, but under the control and management of the municipal corporation. The courts, however, are rapidly departing from this rule, and are taking the view that municipal corporations proper are liable for the management of all property, even of such property as is used in the performance of a purely public or governmental duty. The reasons for such decisions are not, however, generally clearly stated, and do not, in most cases, seem even to be grasped by the courts arriving at the decision. One of the strongest cases holding to this view is that of Galvin v. New York.[1] Here the driver of a cart was injured while delivering coal at the court-house, by a heavy grating, which, being negligently fastened up, fell upon him. In the opinion, Chief Justice Ruger says: "No question arises as to the defendant's negligence, and it was admitted on the trial that it owned the courthouse, and was charged with keeping and maintaining the same and its appurtenances in a safe and suitable condition, free from danger to those lawfully in and about the building." The ownership of the court-house by the city of New York resulted from the fact that the city and the county of New York were one and the same corporation. It was in its capacity as county corporation that the city of New York happened to own the build-

[1] 112 N. Y. 223.

ing about which the negligence occurred. The court, however, makes no allowance for this fact, and bases the liability of the city simply upon the general duty to maintain the property, which it owned and controlled, in proper condition. The court further makes no allowance for the fact that the property about which the negligence occurred, namely, the court-house, was used for a purely public and governmental purpose, and not for the private emolument or advantage of the city which was held responsible for negligence in its management. It thus assumes, without argument, and indeed without citation of cases, that a city is responsible for the management of all its property, making no allowance for the distinction which runs through the entire law of torts, as applicable to municipal corporations, between private and public duties. This case is, therefore, unsatisfactory, however correct the actual decision may be, for the reason that no ground for the decision is stated by the court, but the liability of the municipal corporation is simply assumed.

Another important case holding to this view is that of Briegel v. The City of Philadelphia.[1] This was a case of trespass to recover for injuries to a dwelling-house, caused by the negligence of the city in defectively constructing the plumbing and

[1] 135 Pa. St. 451; 20 American State Reports, 885.

drainage of a public school building, owned and maintained by the city upon its property. The city was held responsible. The reason given for the decision is the ample power and the full liability assigned to municipal corporations. Judge Mitchell distinguishes the case from that of a *quasi*-municipal corporation like a school district in the same conditions. He says: "The learned counsel for the city have made an urgent and ingenious effort to bring this case within the ruling in Ford *v.* Kendall School District.[1] The distinction, however, is plain. That case was an action for the negligence of the janitor of a school building, and was decided on the ground that under the Pennsylvania statutes, school districts are agencies of the commonwealth for a special and limited purpose, with no funds under their control, but public moneys devoted to a specific charity, and not divertible, even indirectly, to any other use. This purpose might be entirely destroyed by holding the funds liable for the consequences of tort by the officers or servants of the school district, and therefore such liability cannot be sustained. . . . The present action differs from the class we have been considering in being against the city of Philadelphia, and in being an action for nuisance by the negligent use of property. The city having a

[1] 121 Pa. St. 543.

general power of taxation, and exercising full municipal functions, comes under the larger measure of liability. . . . In the class of cases to which the present belongs, injuries arising from the misuse of land, there has never been any substantial hesitation in holding cities liable. The ownership of property entails certain burdens, one of which is the obligation that it shall not injure others in their property or person by unlawful use or neglect."

Here again it will be observed that the duty of the municipal corporation to keep its property, of whatever character, private or public, in good condition, is assumed, and the distinction between its position and that of a *quasi*-municipal corporation in similar conditions is found in the fact of the larger financial powers possessed by the municipal corporation proper. No allowance at all is made for the fact that the property was devoted to a public and governmental and not a private and corporate purpose. It will be remembered, however, that in several cases *quasi*-municipal corporations have been held liable where they had assumed duties of a private and corporate nature, and were negligent in their performance, notwithstanding their *quasi*-corporate character.[1] The reasoning adopted by the court in this case of

[1] *Supra*, p. 155.

Briegel *v.* Philadelphia can hardly, therefore, be considered satisfactory.

There are a number of other cases, also, which hold to this view that municipal corporations are responsible for the management of their property, regardless of the fact whether such property is used for public and governmental purposes, and where no reason at all is assigned for the decision. Thus in the case of McCaughey *v.* Tritt,[1] the corporation of Providence was held responsible for injuries to a workman caused in building the city hall. In this case, commissioners had been appointed to build the city hall for the city of Providence, and, through their negligence, the workman was injured. A verdict against the city was sustained, but no reason was assigned for the decision. Particularly was no consideration given to the question of the public character of the building in the erection of which the negligence occurred.

Another case is that of Neuert *v.* The City of Boston.[2] Here the city owned a building to which a wire, which was used by the fire department, was attached. The city had sold the building, which was to be removed. While being removed, the wire had become lowered, and the plaintiff passing on the highway, came in contact with it to his

[1] 12 R. I. 449.   [2] 120 Mass. 339.

injury. The city was held liable, and the ground was its negligence in doing something connected with its property, and not for the purposes of the fire department, which was regarded as a public and governmental institution. It is true that the duty of the municipal corporation to maintain its highways in safe condition might have been regarded as the ground of the decision, but the court preferred to put it upon the ground of its duty to keep its property in good condition.

In another case, Carrington v. The City of St. Louis,[1] the plaintiff, a minor, was injured by falling against the iron trap doors of a cellar-way in a sidewalk in the city of St. Louis. The cellar-way belonged to a police station, and the doors covering it and opening into the police station had been painted by a member of the police force, who, after painting them, propped them open with a stick and left them in that position to dry. The city was held liable for the damages resulting to the plaintiff, but the ground of the liability was found in the duty of the city to keep its streets and sidewalks in a reasonably safe condition. Owing also to a peculiar local statute, which provided that police officers were city officers, it was held that the negligence was that of a city officer, and that therefore the city was responsible for the damages resulting

[1] 89 Missouri, 208; 58 American Reports, 108.

from it. In this case it will be noticed that the property about which the negligence had been committed was a police station which was used for a purpose almost universally recognized as governmental and public, rather than private and local in character. The subject is somewhat complicated, however, by the fact that the doors of the cellarway of this building, through whose opening the damage was caused, opened upon the sidewalk, and the basis of the liability of the city may therefore be found in the negligence of its well-recognized duty to keep its streets in a safe condition.[1]

So far, it must be admitted, we have been unable to find any satisfactory ground for the imposition of a liability upon municipal corporations for negligence in the management of property devoted to a purely public purpose, where such property is not connected with the streets. To find a satisfactory basis for the liability, we must find one which will also apply to the relations of *quasi*-municipal corporations. If the one class of public authorities is to be held liable for property managed and used for a purely public purpose, certainly there is no logical reason for relieving the other class from such liability if we hold both classes liable for mis-

---

[1] See also Greencastle *v.* Martin, 74 Indiana, 449; 39 American Reports, 93, where a city was held liable for negligence in the maintenance of a pound.

management of property used for a purely private and local purpose. It is not meant by this statement to criticise at all the justice of the decisions in accordance with which municipal corporations are held liable for the management of their public property. The attempt is only being made to find out a proper logical basis of the liability. This would seem to have been reached in a case in Indiana, namely, that of Mulcairns *v.* The City of Janesville.[1] In this case the city was engaged in constructing a cistern for the use of the fire department, which is everywhere recognized as a public and governmental rather than a private and corporate institution, and by the negligence of one of its agents a workman was injured. The city was held liable, and the court distinguished the case from those where the negligence was that of officers of the fire department engaged in extinguishing a fire. Here it was said they would be discharging a purely governmental, and not a private and corporate function. The court says: "The distinction between the two cases is very wide and quite apparent; if the city could not be held liable in such a case [as the one at bar] it never could in any, for it is a case, a common case, of special employment for the performance of special services for and in behalf of the city. [The city had employed a par-

[1] 29 N. W. Reporter, 565.

ticular person not a member of the fire department to superintend and manage the construction of the cistern.] It was a legal duty of the city to construct cisterns for fire purposes, and it was engaged in the attempted performance of its duty through its own private agencies and not through the fire department or its officers or other officers of the city whose duty it was to perform the work." The court says also that the cases which were distinguished from the case at bar were based "upon the doctrine generally recognized that when the agents acting for the city are not in the employment of the city, but act rather as public officers, such as the fire department provided for by law, and the city does nothing more than appoint its officers, such persons perform duties fixed by law and not special services contracted to be performed under the employment of the city."

A case decided on somewhat similar principles is that of The City of Lafayette v. Alick.[1] Here it was held without argument, however, and without the citation of cases, that a city was liable where an engineer of its fire department was injured by the bursting of a boiler of one of the fire engines which was defective, the defect being known to the city officers and not to the man injured. In this case, at the time of the injury the fire engine, whose

[1] 81 Indiana, 166.

defective condition, due to the negligence of the city, was the cause of the accident, was not being made use of for the purpose of extinguishing a fire, but for the purpose of pumping water from a cistern into one of the water pipes of the city. Both of these cases seem to make the distinction between the duty of the city to maintain its property in good condition, which is regarded as a private and a local duty, and the duty for the performance of which the property may have been purchased and is being maintained, and which may be public and governmental in character without affecting this private and municipal duty for the negligence of which the city may properly be held responsible.

Mr. Jones, in his excellent monograph on the "Negligence of Municipal Corporations," is the first author upon the subject to attempt the classification under one head of the duties of municipal corporations of this character, whose negligence will lead to a liability for damages. He classes such duties under the general head of "Municipal Duties relating to Governmental Affairs," and embraces within this head not only such duties as the care of property devoted to a public purpose, but also and because of its close connection with property, the duty of maintaining highways and streets and sidewalks and bridges in proper condition, as well as the duty to carry on public improvements in such a way as not to injure individuals. This is, perhaps, the only satisfactory basis for the liability which is imposed upon municipal corporations so generally in this country for the negligence of a long series of duties; but it must be admitted that the classification has not yet approved itself to many of the courts, which still prefer to hold, with certain exceptions for which satisfactory reasons have not as yet been advanced, to the old rule of distinction, namely, the private or public character of the duty at issue, and allow the character of such duty to fix the character of all property held for its performance.[1]

We have thus three separate and distinct grounds assigned by the various courts of this country for the liability of public governmental corporations

[1] A case whose facts are quite similar to those of Lafayette v. Alick came up before the courts of New Jersey, which arrived at the contrary conclusion. This was the case of Wild v. Paterson, 47 N. J. Law, 40. Here it was held, that the city was not liable to a member of the fire department who, while assisting to haul the engine to a fire, was injured because the engine had not a brake in good order. The ground given for the non-liability was that the duty to maintain the fire department is owed to the public and imposed by law; and the court says that the distinction which was sought to be made by the plaintiff that the duty violated, namely, that of keeping the machinery used for extinguishing fires in good order, is a private duty, was specious, and that this duty was plainly included within the general public duty to maintain the fire department. The court held also, that the city was not liable because it did not as a corporation receive from the performance of this duty any special benefit or advantage.

for their management of the public property under their control: The first is found in the character of their corporate capacity. If such corporate capacity be the full corporate capacity which is possessed by municipal corporations proper, they are held liable. If, on the other hand, it be that corporate capacity which is possessed by *quasi*-municipal corporations, they are irresponsible. This basis for the liability, however, does not explain, nor does it afford a good ground for, the rule that *quasi*-municipal corporations are liable for mismanagement of property used for a local or private purpose, nor does it explain the liability which by quite a number of the courts of this country is imposed upon such bodies for the management of highways, a liability which, where it is not recognized by the courts, is now very generally being recognized by statute.

The second ground of the liability of public corporations for the management of their property is to be found in the character of the purpose for which the property is being used. If that purpose is a public or governmental one, the corporation is not regarded as liable; if, on the other hand, it is a private purpose for the emolument and advantage of the corporation, the liability is recognized. This rule of liability does not, however, explain the cases (cases which are increasing in number all the time) where municipal corporations proper are held responsible for the management of property which is used for a purely public purpose.

The third ground of the liability of public corporations for the management of their property is to be found in the rule that the duty to maintain property, for whatever purpose it may be used, in a safe condition, is not connected with government in the sense that the municipal corporation is then to share in the immunity of the government for tort, but that this duty is a duty of a local and private character easily distinguishable from the governmental purpose for which the property may be used. This is the only basis for this liability which is satisfactory. The rule of liability founded upon it is the only one which is at once just and logical. It explains, at the same time, the cases where municipal corporations proper are held liable for the management of property used by them as agents of the general government of the country, and the cases where *quasi*-municipal corporations are held liable for the management of property devoted to their private uses and for the management of highways, if we recognize that highways are property.

Its complete adoption will result in furthering the cause of justice, in that *quasi*-municipal corporations will be held liable for negligence in the management of public property more generally than they have been so held in the past.

The confusion in the law upon this general subject of the torts of municipal corporations, and public corporations generally, is due very largely to the attempt to transfer into the law relative to these bodies the principle of the irresponsibility of the state, a principle which results from the non-recognition of the corporate liability of the state. This failure to recognize the liability of the state arises, however, not from the failure to recognize its corporate character, for it has been held that even in the absence of express provision by statute or the constitution, the state both may make contracts and suffer wrongs, and may therefore maintain in its corporate name actions to enforce its rights and redress its injuries,[1] and is theoretically liable on its contracts,[2] but from the assumed impolicy of admitting that the government, the representative of the sovereign, can do a legal wrong for which it may be held liable.

It has been shown, however,[3] that considerations of public policy do not demand that the liability of the government for tort shall never be recognized, but only that the government shall not

---

[1] Delahey v. Illinois, 2 Hill, N. Y. 162; Indiana v. Worann, 6 Hill, N. Y. 33.

[2] *Supra*, p. 106.   [3] *Supra*, p. 114.

be liable for torts resulting from the exercise of its purely authoritative or sovereign functions. If this is true of the position of the state, if the logic of the law, as the law of France and Germany would seem to show, does not require that the state should be held irresponsible where it enters into private relations with an individual, how much more necessary is it in the case of these *quasi*-public bodies, such as municipal corporations, and even *quasi*-municipal corporations, to recognize that when they enter into private relations they should be held to all of the duties imposed upon individuals by the private law. We may indeed recognize the desire shown in the later decisions of the courts to hold municipal corporations proper, and even in some cases *quasi*-municipal corporations, more strictly to their duty in the management of property, for whatever purpose it may be devoted, as an evidence of that general tendency, which one cannot fail to remark in the entire American administrative law, to subject the agencies of government more fully than formerly to a judicial control, and particularly to seize hold of any opportunity to impose upon the various governmental authorities not only a corporate capacity to be used for their advantage, but also a corporate liability to be enforced for the protection of the private rights of individuals. We have already recognized the liability of the state for contracts made with individuals, through the organization of special jurisdictions before which claims on such contracts made against the state may be determined or through the power given to the ordinary courts to hold the state responsible for the contracts which it may have entered into with individuals. We have also very generally assigned a corporate character to our localities. This, in a country as decentralized as is our own, has resulted in the subjection of almost all of the contracts, into which the state may enter, to the control of the courts. We have further recognized with regard to the various local corporations through which so much of the work of the state is done, that in so far as they do not discharge governmental functions, and the idea of governmental function is being continually narrowed, they are also responsible for torts. May we not hope that with the extension of this principle of the liability for torts of the lesser agencies of the government, the government as a whole may in its purely private legal relations in time be held to the same responsibility to which individuals are held, a responsibility which has been shown not only is required by the logic of our law, but also should be introduced as a result of the experience of other countries.

The strong desire, manifested by the courts in their decisions, to protect private rights, has thus led them in their more recent utterances to abandon more and more the idea that the governmental position of municipal corporations, and even of public corporations as a whole, is to relieve them from liability for damages caused by their negligence to care for property placed in their control. While we cannot censure the adoption of this course, while, indeed, we must give it our approval, we are still obliged to admit that this fact does, from the point of view of the work undertaken in these pages, render the more recent decisions of the courts upon the particular point almost valueless. For if the idea is adopted, as it would seem to be, that public corporations are liable for their management of all property, no room is left for a distinction between public and governmental property, and private or corporate property.

CHAPTER IX

WHAT MUNICIPAL PROPERTY IS PROTECTED BY THE CONSTITUTIONAL PROVISIONS PROTECTING PRIVATE PROPERTY

The courts are not only inclining towards recognizing all property of municipal corporations as so far private as to give a claim for damages in case individuals are injured by the negligence of the corporation in its management, or, to speak more exactly, the courts are not only recognizing more and more, that the duty to care for property is a municipal or private duty, distinguishable in character from the duty for the performance of which the property may be held, and are more and more inclining towards holding the corporation liable for its improper performance. They are also more and more recognizing, that from the point of view of the inviolable private rights of municipal corporations, these bodies may hold property as private in character, and therefore as inviolable in character by any governmental action as the property of individuals. It is indeed true that this position has not been reached without considerable reluctance.¹ This reluctance has been caused by the fear that a recognition of the private property rights of municipal corporations would put them in a position of too great independence over against the legislature, the only guardian in our decentralized system of administration of the uniform and harmonious action of the administration. It has also been justified by the undeniable fact that almost all of the duties of municipal corporations affect the public, or at any rate that portion of the public which resides within their limits, and that consequently the property held by municipal corporations to aid them in the performance of these duties is really different from the property of private individuals.

This reluctance has, however, finally been overcome, it is believed, by a consideration of the position into which our system of constitutional restrictions with its resulting lessening of legislative responsibility has forced the courts. For just as our legislatures have been made the guardians of administrative uniformity and harmony, so the courts have, through the exercise of their power of enforcing constitutional limitations, become the guardians of those private rights guaranteed by the

[1] See remarks of Judge Denio, Darlington v. New York, 31 N. Y. 164; 87 American Decisions, 248.

constitution, whether those rights are possessed by individuals or by private or public corporations.

We find thus in some of the earliest decisions of the United States Supreme Court, a recognition of the private character of certain of the property of municipal corporations, *i.e.* the property owned by them in fee and used for purposes of revenue, and *dicta* very strong in character to the effect that such private property is not capable of being divested by the action of the legislature. The first case in which we find such a *dictum* is that of Terrett and others *v.* Taylor and others.[1] Here the United States Supreme Court says: "In respect also to public corporations which exist only for public purposes, such as counties, towns, cities, etc., the legislature may, under proper limitations, have a right to change, modify, enlarge, or restrain them, securing, however, the property for the use of those for whom and at whose expense it was originally purchased." Again, in the case of Town of Pawlet *v.* Clark and others[2] we find the following: "By the operation of these statutes and especially of that of 1794, which, so far as it granted the glebes to the towns, could not afterwards be repealed by the legislature so as to divest the right of the towns under the grant, the towns respec-

---

[1] 9 Cranch, 43. the *dictum* being found on p. 52.
[2] *Ibid.* 292, 230.

tively became entitled to all the glebes situated therein which had not been previously appropriated by the regular and legal erection of an Episcopal Church within the particular town." Finally, in the great case of Dartmouth College *v.* Woodward[1] Mr. Justice Story says: "But it will hardly be contended that even in respect to such [that is, public corporations], the legislative power is so transcendent that it may, at its will, take away the private property of the corporation or change the uses of its private funds acquired under the public faith. Can the legislature confiscate to its own use the private funds which a municipal corporation holds under its charter without any default or consent of the corporators? If a municipal corporation be capable of holding devises and legacies to charitable uses (as many municipal corporations are), does the legislature under our forms of limited government possess the authority to seize upon those funds and appropriate them to other uses at its arbitrary pleasure against the will of the donors and donees? From the very nature of our government the public faith is pledged the other way, and that pledge constitutes a valid contract, and that contract is subject only to judicial inquiry, construction, and abrogation. This court has already had occasion in other causes to

[1] 4 Wheaton, 518, 694.

express its opinion on this subject, and there is not the slightest inclination to retract it."[1] Notwithstanding this strong enunciation of the principle of the inviolability of the private property of municipal corporations, it must be noticed that the reason which Mr. Justice Story gives for the adoption of the rule, is not so much the fact that the municipal corporations themselves are to be protected, as the fact that they may hold property in trust as a result of a devise made by some private individual, and it would appear that this is the private property to which he refers in this statement. It is the devise of some individual that is to be protected rather than the property right of the corporation. This *dictum* of Judge Story was followed by the court of Vermont in the case of Montpelier *v.* East Montpelier.[2] By a charter dating from colonial times, the government had granted to the town of Montpelier, certain property to be held in trust for the support of a clergyman and for divine worship in the town, and also for the use and support of English schools. By a statute passed in the year 1848, the legislature divided the town of Montpelier into two new towns, one called Montpelier, the

---

[1] Here Mr. Justice Story refers to the cases of Terrett *v.* Taylor, and Town of Pawlet *v.* Clark, already referred to above.

[2] 29 Vermont, 12.

other East Montpelier. In making this division the legislature made no provision for the disposition of the trust estate, and appointed no one to take charge of these public land rights, and to collect and expend the rents. The town of East Montpelier having collected and expended a considerable amount of the rents and profits from the land, the larger part of which was situated within the limits of the new town of East Montpelier, the town of Montpelier prayed that the town of East Montpelier be ordered to pay over all money it had collected as rents, and that it be perpetually enjoined from the further collection thereof and interference therewith, that a trustee be appointed with authority to take charge of, control, and manage such lands and rents, and that such trustee be instructed by the Chancellor as to the mode of appropriating such trust funds. The Chancellor issued a decree dismissing the bill, and appeal was taken from such decree to the Supreme Court of the state. This body decided that the decree of the Chancellor must be reversed and the case remanded to the Court of Chancery, with directions to appoint a trustee or trustees of the trust property and appropriate the same as directed in the original charter. In rendering the opinion of the court, Judge Isham admits that it is perfectly proper for the legislature to destroy the old town of Montpelier, and in this way practically to destroy the trustee of this trust notwithstanding that it would have been incompetent for the legislature to remove an individual private trustee from his trust. He makes a distinction between a private trustee and a municipal corporation as a trustee, basing his distinction upon the fact that the municipal corporation was organized for the purpose of aiding the state in maintaining its form of government, and that the power must therefore necessarily reside in the state to abolish that organization when it ceases to have that effect. Judge Isham admits further that the legislature has the power to divide a town and to apportion its public property, that is, property held for strictly governmental purposes, in such manner as it sees fit, as the result of its general powers of control over all governmental agencies, but he also asserts that, "it has as uniformly been held that towns and other public corporations may have private rights and interests vested in them under their charter; and as to those rights they are to be regarded and protected the same as if they were the rights and interests of individuals or of private corporations; and grants of property to them in trust for other purposes than corporate and municipal use are no more the subject of legislative control than are the private and vested rights of individuals. . . . The statute constitutionally directed a division of the property held by the town of Montpelier under its original charter in their corporate and municipal capacity, and which was to be applied for municipal purposes, but it had no effect upon this property held by them in trust for the specific purposes mentioned in the charter and which was not designed for their use as a municipal corporation."

To a similar effect is the case of People v. Ingersoll.[1] In this case certain persons occupying official positions, had, it was alleged, fraudulently misappropriated moneys belonging to the city and county of New York; and the attempt was made by the state to bring suit against them in order to recover back such moneys. The question to be decided by the Court of Appeals of the state of New York, was whether the state was a proper party to the suit, and it was held that it was not, inasmuch as the property which it was alleged had been fraudulently misappropriated, belonged not to the state, but to the municipal corporation, and that, therefore, the municipal corporation was the only party which might bring suit to recover the money; that the relation of principal and agent does not exist be-

[1] 58 N. Y. 1.

tween the state and a municipal corporation, in respect to the exercise of corporate functions; and that the money raised by municipal corporations for corporate purposes does not belong to the state, either in the capacity of trustee, principal, or owner. Judge Allen, who delivered the opinion of the court, says: " In political and governmental matters, the municipalities are the representatives of the sovereignty of the state, and auxiliary to it; in other matters relating to property rights, pecuniary obligations, they have the attributes and distinctive legal rights of private corporations, and may acquire property, create debts, and sue, and be sued, as other corporations, and in the borrowing of money, and incurring pecuniary obligations in any form, as well as in the buying and selling of property within the limits of the corporate powers conferred, they neither represent nor bind the state." The judge goes on to say that municipal corporations hold all such property, as trustees for the inhabitants, within the territorial limits of the corporation, including taxpayers and non-taxpayers, and that the money obtained by the issue of bonds or by the levy of taxes, is a trust fund for public use by the corporate authority, and belongs to the municipal treasury.[1]

[1] A similar case, and one decided about the same time, is that of People v. Fields, 58 N. Y. 491.

But while the legislature may not deprive the inhabitants of the use of property left in trust for them, it may still, in the exercise of its supervisory powers over municipal corporations, change the trustee if it sees fit, where such trustee is a municipal corporation. This is intimated in the opinion in the case of Montpelier *v.* East Montpelier, just referred to, and is held to be perfectly proper in Philadelphia *v.* Fox.[1] Here it was provided by statute that the city of Philadelphia, which had been made a trustee for charitable purposes, should cease to be trustee, and that certain persons, viz., the mayor, presidents of the city councils, and twelve citizens to be appointed by the courts within the city and county of Philadelphia, should act as trustees. This act was held to be a perfectly proper exercise of the control possessed by the legislature over municipal corporations, and not to deprive the *cestuis que trustent*, *i.e.* the inhabitants of the city, of their rights which were left intact.[2] Further, the inviolability of municipal property does not interfere with the principle that the legislature has in the absence of express constitutional provision, absolute control over the boundaries of municipal corporations; may thus divide or extend the boundaries of

---

[1] 64 Pa. St. 169.
[2] See also Girard *v.* Philadelphia, 7 Wallace, 1.

municipal corporations,[1] and, as a result, may distribute among the new corporations formed, the public property belonging to the old corporation, in an equitable manner.[2]

But there are numerous cases which recognize not only that the legislature may not take away from the inhabitants of municipal corporations the use and benefits of property held in trust for them, but also that municipal corporations themselves may not be deprived by the legislature of property of a private character held by them in fee.

Thus, in Town of Milwaukee *v.* City of Milwaukee,[3] it was held that an act of the legislature annexing to a city part of a town did not divest the town of land contained in the annexed district to which it had the exclusive title. The reason for the decision was, that the legislature could not take such action without obtaining the consent of the town, and Chief Justice Dixon, in delivering the opinion of the court, says: "The difficulty about the question is to distinguish between the corporation as a civil institution or delegation of merely political power, and as an ideal being

---

[1] Laramie County *v.* Albany County, 92 U. S. 307, 311.
[2] Town of Milwaukee *v.* City of Milwaukee, 12 Wisconsin, 93; Morgan *v.* Beloit, 7 Wall. 613, 617.
[3] 12 Wisconsin, 93.

endowed with the capacity to acquire and hold property for corporate and other purposes. In its political or governmental capacity, it is liable at any time to be changed, modified, or destroyed by the legislature; but in its capacity of owner of property, designed for its own or the exclusive use and benefit of its inhabitants, its vested rights of property are no more the subject of legislative interference or control without the consent of the corporators, than those of a merely private corporation or person. Its rights of property, once acquired, though designed and used to aid it in the discharge of its duties as a local government, are entirely distinct and separate from its powers as a political or municipal body." The judge admits, however, that on the division of a municipal corporation, the legislature might provide for a fair and equitable disposition of its public property.

To the same effect is the case of Grogan *v.* San Francisco.[1] Here the legislature attempted by statute to ratify an imperfect conveyance of wharves made by the city, and made no provision for a ratification of such validating act by the city or its authorities. The court held that the legislature could not do this, inasmuch as it was practically an attempt to convey by legislation

[1] 18 California, 590.

the property of the city. Judge Field, in rendering the decision of the court, said: "The estate, having vested in the city, ceased to be subject to the legislation of the state except to the same extent that all property is thus subject. It could not afterwards be divested by the state, or by any proceedings instituted by her direction. . . . Nor is there any difference in the inviolability of a contract between a grant of property to an individual and a like grant to a municipal corporation. So far as municipal corporations are invested with subordinate legislative powers for local purposes, they are mere instrumentalities of the state for the convenient administration of the government, and their powers are under the entire control of the legislature; they may be qualified, enlarged, restricted, or withdrawn, at its discretion. But these bodies, says Kent, 'may also be empowered to take and hold private property for municipal uses, and such property is invested with the security of other private rights.' . . . And though a municipal corporation is the creature of the legislature, yet, when the state enters into a contract with it, the subordinate relation ceases, and that equality arises which exists between all contracting parties, and however great the control of the legislature over a corporation, it can be exercised only in subordination to the principle which secures the inviolability of contracts." [1]

The most recent and one of the strongest cases upon the subject is Mount Hope Cemetery v. The City of Boston.[2] Here the legislature of the state of Massachusetts had provided for the organization of the Mount Hope Cemetery Company, and had also provided that the city of Boston should convey to such cemetery company all the lands constituting the cemetery, together with the stocks, tools, implements, and other personal property appertaining thereto or commonly used thereon. The question came up upon a *mandamus* to compel the city of Boston and its mayor to transfer such cemetery to the cemetery company, and the court refused to issue it, considering that this act was not a proper exercise of the legislative control over municipal corporations, inasmuch as it was an attempt to require the transfer of private property without compensation, and was contrary both to the constitution of the United States and to that of Massachusetts. The opinion is given by Judge Allen, who says that : "By a quite general concurrence of opinion . . . this legislative power of control is not universal and does not extend to

---

[1] There is a series of similar cases, known as the City Slip cases, in which this rule of law is applied.

[2] 158 Mass. 509.

property acquired by a city or town for special purposes not deemed strictly and exclusively public and political, but in respect to which a city or town is deemed rather to have a right of private ownership of which it cannot be deprived against its will save by the right of eminent domain with payment of compensation. . . . In this commonwealth the question has not directly arisen in reference to the power of the legislature to compel a transfer of the property of a city or town, but the double character of cities and towns in reference to their duties and liabilities has very often been adverted to. . . . The conclusion to which we have come is, that the cemetery falls within the class of property which the city owns in its private or proprietary character as a private corporation might own it, and that its ownership is protected under the constitutions of Massachusetts and of the United States, so that the legislature has no power to require its transfer without compensation." Judge Allen claims also for the city a right of private property in many other kinds of municipal property. He says: "The city of Boston is possessed of much other property which, in a certain sense, and to a certain extent, is held for the benefit of the public, but in other respects is held more like the property of a private corporation. Notably among these may be mentioned its system of water works, its system of parks, its markets, its hospital, and its library. In establishing all of these the city has not acted strictly as an agent of the state government for the accomplishment of general public or political purposes, but with special reference to the benefit of its own inhabitants. If its cemetery is under legislative control, so that a transfer of it without compensation can be required, it is not easy to see why the other properties mentioned are not also; and all the other cities and towns which own cemeteries or other properties of the kinds mentioned might be under a similar liability." There are other cases which either directly hold or intimate that parks are in the nature of private property. The most important case upon this point is the case of People *v.* The Common Council of Detroit.[1]

Further, it has been held that where the legislature has granted to a municipal corporation the

---

[1] 28 Michigan, 228, already commented on. See also State *v.* Schweickardt, 19 South-Western Reporter, 47. See also People *v.* Mayor of Chicago, 51 Illinois, 17. But the contrary is held in David *v.* Portland Water Commissioners, 14 Oregon, 98, where the court says: "Public parks, gas, water, and sewerage in towns and cities may ordinarily be classed as private affairs, but they often become matters of public importance, and when the legislature determines that there is a public necessity for their use in a certain locality, I do not think they can be designated as mere private affairs. That is a relative question." See also Burrell *v.* Tacoma, 8 Washington, 156; 40 American State Reports, 895.

right to build wharves and to charge wharfage, and the city has in pursuance of such law expended large sums of money in the construction of wharves, the legislature may not subsequently provide that certain classes of vessels shall not be obliged to pay wharfage rates. For the rights of the corporation under such a statute are private rights protected by the constitution.[1]

While all of these cases would seem to recognize that it is possible for municipal corporations to own property distinct and apart from their position as governmental agents, none of them actually decides the point that such property is free from legislative control in the same way as is ordinary private property. There are, however, not a few cases which decide this point definitely. One of the best is Benson v. The Mayor.[2] In this case the question came up as to the right which New York city possessed in the ferries. The facts were as follows: New York city had been granted certain ferry rights by the original colonial charters, and in pursuance of such charters had granted to a ferry company the right to operate certain ferries. The legislature of the state of New York thereafter provided for the appointment of certain com-

---

[1] Ellerman v. McMains, 30 La. Ann. 190; 31 American Reports, 218, approved in N. O. M. & T. R. R. Co. v. Ellerman, 105 U. S. 166.
[2] 10 Barbour, N. Y. 223.

missioners to lease these ferries belonging to the city, and the lessees of such commissioners had applied to the Supreme Court for an injunction to restrain the corporation of the city of New York from executing the leases which it had itself made of these ferries. The court refused to issue the injunction, and in the course of the opinion it was said: "Franchises of this description are partly of a public and partly of a private nature. So far as the accommodation of passengers is concerned, they are *publici juris;* so far as they require capital and produce revenues, they are *privati juris.* Certain duties and burdens are imposed upon the grantees, who are compensated therefor by the privilege of levying ferriage, and the security from spoliation arising from the irrevocable nature of the grant. The state may legislate touching them so far as they are *publici juris.* Thus laws may be passed to punish neglect or misconduct in conducting the ferries, to secure the safety of passengers from danger, imposition, etc. But the state cannot take away the ferries themselves nor deprive the city of their legitimate rents and profits. The franchise, however, may be forfeited by non-user judicially ascertained, and the government, in the exercise of the sovereign power of eminent domain, may resume the property for public use on making a just compensation, but not otherwise." In another place the judge says: "The city of New York and its inhabitants have acquired vested rights and valuable interests in these ferries, which cannot be taken away by the legislature." It has sometimes been intimated that this decision is not in accord with the rule of the United States Supreme Court in the case of Town of East Hartford *v.* The Hartford Bridge Co.[1] If, however, this case is carefully examined, it will be seen that it can hardly be said that such is the case. In this case the legislature had, upon the incorporation of the town of East Hartford, granted to it one-half of the ferry over the Connecticut River *during the pleasure of the General Assembly.* Several years later a company was incorporated to build a bridge across this river, which, being erected, the legislature resolved that the ferry should be discontinued. The Supreme Court of the United States held that the act discontinuing the ferry was not inconsistent with that part of the Constitution which forbids the states from passing any law impairing the obligation of contract. The fact that the grant was made during the pleasure of the legislature is sufficient to account for the decision, but, although it had an effect upon it, it must be admitted that the court, in its opinion, claimed the power for the legislature

[1] 10 Howard, 511.

because this was a matter of public, rather than of private, law.[1]

A very strong case upon the right of municipal corporations to manage their property free from legislative control is that of Webb *v.* The Mayor of New York.[2] In this case the legislature attempted, without the consent of the city of New York, to provide that the land occupied by the present Forty-second Street reservoir should be used for the purposes of a public park or square. The result of the act, had it been upheld, would have been to make property from which the city was deriving a revenue useless for that purpose. An injunction was applied for to prevent the carrying out of the provisions of the statute, and Judge Macomber held that this was a violation of the provisions of the United States and the state constitutions preventing the legislature from taking property for public use without giving compensation. The judge, in rendering his opinion, lays particular stress on the peculiar position of the city of New York and on the fact that this property had come to it from a grant of the English Crown, and had been given to it in absolute fee. This, of

---

[1] But see Roper *v.* McWhorter, 77 Virginia, 214, which holds definitely that ferry franchises are public property, and may be resumed at any time by the legislature.

[2] 64 Howard's Practice, 10.

course, is not the case with many cities, either in the state of New York or in other states, and is to be regarded as somewhat weakening the force of the decision as applicable to ordinary municipal corporations.[1]

There are several cases also which go even further than to protect private property, and claim a similar protection for all property of municipal corporations. One of the most marked of these is that of Spaulding v. Andover.[2] In this case the legislature had, by an act of 1870, granted to the town of Andover a certain number of bonds to be devoted to the reimbursement of the expenditures incurred by the town for military bounties. The court said: "This was an unqualified, unlimited, unincumbered grant, possessing all the incidents of an executed and irrevocable contract.... The law of 1872 [whose constitutionality has been called in question], declaring a portion of the fund which had been solemnly granted to the town of Andover to belong to and be the property of certain individuals [those who had been counted as being part of the quota of the town, but had never received any bounty from the town], is invalid as

---

[1] But see Coyle v. McIntire, 7 Houston, Delaware, 44, which denies to the legislature the right to appoint water commissioners who are to receive and collect all water rents and manage the water works of a city.

[2] 54 N. H. 38, 56.

being contrary to that provision of the Federal Constitution, Article I., Section 10, which declares that no state shall pass a law impairing the obligation of contracts." In this case it will be noticed that the property, namely, the bonds which were granted to the town, were not granted with the expectation that it should derive revenue therefrom, or that they should be used for specifically municipal purposes, but they were granted to reimburse the town for expenses which it had incurred in a purely public matter, namely, the encouragement of enlistment in the army at the time of the civil war. Notwithstanding this public character of the grant, the court held that the grant was so fully an executed contract that it could not be disturbed by subsequent legislation. To a somewhat similar effect is State v. Haven.[1] Here it was held that the legislature could not appropriate money in a city treasury which had been raised by taxation for the purpose of building a high school to the purchase of a site for a normal school in the city, which was a state institution, and Chief Justice Dixon, in rendering the opinion of the court, says, on pages 665 and 666: "It is well settled as to all matters pertaining to vested rights of property, whether real or personal, and to the obligation of contracts, that municipal corporations

[1] 22 Wisconsin, 660.

are as much within the protection of the Federal Constitution as private individuals are. The legislature cannot divest a municipal corporation of its property without the consent of its inhabitants, nor impair the obligation of a contract entered into with or in behalf of such corporations."

A very similar case is Milam Co. *v.* Bateman.[1] Here the legislature of the state of Texas had granted to Milam County certain lands for school purposes, and subsequently, by a special act, provided that patents for such lands, which had been issued to private individuals, and about which there had been some litigation, should be valid, thus destroying the title of the county. It was held that this statute was unconstitutional, on the ground that the property rights of counties were protected by the same constitutional guaranties which shield the property of individuals. "If given for a specific object, the state may, very properly, as in the instance under consideration of our school lands granted to counties, exercise such supervision and control over the actions of the counties as to compel proper execution of the trust or prevent its being defeated; but it is believed that this control, unless by the consent of a county, should be subject to the restriction that the purpose for which the property was originally

[1] 54 Texas, 153, 166.

acquired, shall, as far as circumstances will admit, be kept in view, and that it shall not arbitrarily be diverted, as in the case before us, to private parties, or to wholly different purposes."

It will be noticed that all of the cases, to which reference has been made, have decided that the legislature may not appropriate, without the consent of the municipal corporation, private property belonging to it, that is, property not of a specifically governmental or political character. One or two of the cases, as has been pointed out, go further than this, and claim that the legislature may not divest even property belonging to municipal corporations used for a public or governmental purpose. The rule, however, sustained by the greater weight of authority is, that as to public property the legislature has an almost unlimited control, provided such control is not attempted to be asserted in a way to devote such property to private uses after its dedication to public uses. Thus the legislature may provide that the streets of a municipal corporation, even if owned in fee by the corporation, may, without its consent, and without giving it compensation, be used for a street railway.[1]

[1] People *v.* Kerr, 27 N. Y. 188; Mercer *v.* Pittsburgh Railroad Co., 36 Penn. St. 99; Clinton *v.* Cedar Rapids Railroad Co., 24 Iowa, 455.

Further, property acquired by a municipality through the exercise of the power of taxation, delegated to it by the state, and used by the corporation rather as an agent of the state government than as a *quasi*-private corporation, is still subject to the control of the legislature. Thus the legislature may provide for a centralization of the administration of the police under commissioners of police to be appointed by the central administrative authorities of the state, and may require the municipal corporation to transfer to such police commissioners all property used for the purpose of the police, such as station-houses.[1]

[1] See Mayor of Baltimore *v.* State, 15 Maryland, 576; People *v.* Draper, 15 N. Y. 532; and State *v.* County Court of St. Louis, 34 Missouri, 546. See also Essex Public Road Board *v.* Skinkle, 140 U. S. 304, in which it was held that the legislature might provide for the sale of land purchased by a public road board which could not acquire a proprietary interest in such land, both because it was a merely *quasi*-public corporation, and because the land had been acquired for a public governmental purpose, and was, therefore, under the control of the legislature. On the general subject of the control of the legislature over the property of municipal corporations, see the monographic note to 35 American State Reports, p. 529. Among these cases should be mentioned Darlington *v.* Mayor, 31 N. Y. 164; 87 American Decisions, 248, in which Judge Denio claims for the legislature supreme powers of control over all municipal property.

CHAPTER X

WHAT MUNICIPAL PROPERTY IS SUBJECT TO ALIENATION

The reluctance which the courts have had to decide that municipal property may be private in character so as to be incapable of being divested by legislative action — a reluctance which in some cases, it must be admitted, they have allowed themselves too easily to overcome — has been greater when they have been called upon to decide as to the character of municipal property from the point of view of the power of the corporation to alien or dispose of it. This reluctance, however, is easily understood; for while the courts are, indeed, under our system of government, the protectors of private rights, among which are to be included as well the rights of municipal corporations as those of private individuals, they are at the same time the protectors of the people who form the municipal corporation, who are liable to be injured by the improvident actions of their representatives in the disposition of municipal property.

The American and English law has, from a very early time, recognized that municipal corporations have the power to dispose of their property.[1] From an early time also, the property of municipal corporations, from the point of view of their power to dispose of it, was distinguished as public and private. As to the former, the power was denied in the absence of special legislative permission ; as to the latter, it was admitted. One of the strongest as well as one of the earliest cases decided by the American courts, holding that public property may not be aliened by municipal corporations, is that of Augusta v. Perkins.[2] In this case land had, in the year 1797, been condemned on the motion of its proprietor, and vested in town trustees with power to lay it off into lots and streets with a public square, or common, in the centre. In 1805 the trustees conveyed, for a nominal consideration, to the justices of the county, for the use of the county, a public square which had been formed in accordance with the terms of the law of 1797. The courts of the county were held for quite a time in the

---

[1] See Smith v. Barrett & Clifford, 1 Siderfin, 161, 162, decided in the fifteenth year of the reign of Charles II. In this case it is said in the quaint legal French of the period: " *Nota ;* fuit agree per touts que a cest jour Corporation de Maior & Cominalty ou de Baylius, Burgesses &c. poent per lour Common Seale grant lour terres &c. pur vie ou ans ou en fée, et ceo serra bone & liera lour Successors."   [2] 3 B. Monroe, Kentucky, 437.

buildings erected on this square. Other public buildings were likewise erected thereon. In 1838 the seat of justice was removed from the town of Augusta, and the legislature provided for the sale of the land and buildings at public auction. The land was sold in pursuance thereof and a deed given; and an action of ejectment was brought by the trustees of Augusta against the grantee under the deed. It was decided that the title to the land did not pass by the deed of 1805, inasmuch as the trustees could not alien such public property as a square even to such public officials as the justices of the county. The effect of the deed of 1805 to the county justices was, it was held, to vest in them a control and possession of the public square for the use of the county, and was so far perfectly proper but did not convey the title.[1] In the application of this rule it has been held that all property is public which has been dedicated to a public use, or which is affected by a public trust. Thus not only are streets and public squares so public

---

[1] To the same effect is Alves' Executors *v.* Henderson, 16 B. Monroe, Kentucky, 131. See also the case of Still *v.* Trustees of Lansingburgh, 16 Barbour, N. Y. 107. This was a case of a conveyance of a public square to a church which was held to be of no value. The same rule is adopted in the case of Ransom *v.* Boal, 29 Iowa, 68. This is also the rule of the United States Supreme Court. See Clark *et al.*, Administrators of Milo Hoadley, *v.* San Francisco, 134 U. S. 639.

that they may not be aliened by municipal corporations without legislative authorization, but also commons, greens, and public parks.[1] It has, however, been held that property which may have been bought for a public purpose, as for the erection of public buildings, if not actually used for that purpose, may be sold, inasmuch as it is not regarded as affected by a public trust.[2] It would seem also that wharves are of such a public character that they may not be aliened in the absence of legislative permission.[3] It has been held, on the other hand, as some of the cases already cited would seem to indicate, that land, the fee of which is owned by the city, free of any trust or public use, may be aliened by the city as it sees fit;[4] and that munic-

---

[1] State v. Woodward, 23 Vermont, 92; Brooklyn Park Commissioners v. Armstrong, 45 N. Y. 234, in which it is admitted that lands bought for a park are held in trust for that purpose and may not be sold without the consent of the legislature. This last case is, it must be confessed, in the nature rather of a *dictum* than of an actual decision upon this point.

[2] Conrad v. Rogers, 70 Wisconsin, 492; Beach v. Haynes, 12 Vermont, 15. See also Supervisors of Warren County v. Patterson, 56 Illinois, 111. In this case it was held that a clause in a contract of sale and in a deed of property indicating that the land is sold for a "court-house and other public buildings," does not dedicate it to the public or restrict the right of alienation possessed by the corporation to which the land was deeded.

[3] Matthews v. City of Alexandria, 68 Missouri, 115. See also Lord v. Oconto, 47 Wisconsin, 386.

[4] Kings County Insurance Company v. Stevens, 101 N. Y. 411.

ipal, or even *quasi*-municipal, corporations may sell personal property owned by them, as, for example, shares of stock in a railway company.[1]

Municipal property may be aliened not only voluntarily, but also involuntarily, that is, in execution of a judgment against the corporation. Judge Dillon says:[2] "On principle in the absence of statutable provisions or legislative policy in the particular state, it would seem to be a sound view to hold that the right to contract and the power to be sued give to the creditor the right to recover judgment; that judgment should be enforceable by execution against the strictly private property of the corporation, but not against property owned or used by the corporation for public purposes." In some of the states, however, the rule is that execution may not be levied against any of the property of a public corporation, but that judgments obtained against the corporation shall be enforced by *mandamus*.

We have therefore another means of determining what is the private property of municipal corporations; that is, by a consideration of the

---

[1] See Board *v.* Reynolds, 44 Indiana, 509; Semmes *v.* Columbus, 19 Georgia, 471; Shannon *v.* O'Boyle, 51 Indiana, 565. Of course, if the sale is improvident, it may be set aside by the courts. See Terre Haute *v.* Terre Haute Water Works Company, 70 Indiana, 305.

[2] *Law of Municipal Corporations*, 4th ed., p. 674.

decisions in those states which permit execution to be levied against such property. The state where the decisions are the most numerous upon this point is that of Louisiana, which from a very early time has recognized this principle, the recognition being probably due to the strong influence in that state of the Roman and the French law. Here it is held, in the first place, that taxes or claims for taxes due to the municipal corporation are not to be regarded as private property, and are not, therefore, subject to execution or to garnishment whether in the possession of the municipality itself or in process of collection.[1]

It has further been held in Louisiana that execution may not levy against public buildings with their furniture, such as a court-house, the clerk's office, recorder's office, and jail of any parish within the state;[2] nor against property dedicated for public use, as, for example, land granted to the parish as a site for a court-house, even if a part of

[1] Edgerton v. The Third Municipality of New Orleans, 1 La. Ann. 435; Municipality No. 3 v. Hart, 6 La. Ann. 570. See also Meriwether v. Garrett, 102 U. S. 472; and Brown v. Gates, 16 W. V. 131. This latter case was very well considered, and collects and reviews almost all of the cases decided in this country upon the sale on execution of municipal property and the garnishment of money in the hands of both the corporation for debts due third persons by it and in the hands of third persons for debts due the corporation.

[2] Police Jury of West Baton Rouge v. Michel, 4 La. Ann. 84.

the land, which is not occupied by the actual site of the court-house, is leased, and revenue derived from it.[1]

The exemption of public buildings and property devoted to public use from taxation is carried so far that it is held that the rent of property which has been given for the use, for example, of schools is not subject to execution.[2] The same principle as to the exemption of public buildings and property dedicated to public use has been adopted in Missouri and Indiana. Thus school buildings and the lands on which they were situated, as well as the furniture of the schools, and a square of land dedicated for a city market, were held both exempt from execution to satisfy a judgment against the Board of Education, and not subject to a mechanics' lien.[3] Nor, in case public

---

[1] Police Jury of Plaquemines *v.* Foulhouze *et al.*, 30 La. Ann. 64.

[2] Kline *v.* The Parish of Ascension, 33 La. Ann. 562. See also the case of The New Orleans and the Carrollton Railroad Company *v.* Municipality No. 1, 7 La. Ann. 148, which holds that perpetual ground rents received from land originally a part of the commons of the city could not be seized on execution. The reason given by the court in this case was that the charter of the city contemplated the existence and the maintenance of certain permanent sources of revenue which were provided for the expenses of the government, and authorized taxation only for a deficiency, and that this perpetual revenue of the city for the maintenance of government could not be seized on execution.

[3] See State *v.* Tiedman, 69 Missouri, 306; Abercrombie *v.* Ely,

buildings which have been insured are burned down, may the money received from the policy of insurance be seized on execution.[1] Water works are, from this point of view, regarded as public property and not subject to execution.[2] The public character of water works is carried so far that in Pennsylvania, even in the hands of private water companies, they are not subject to a mechanics' lien,[3] although they are regarded when in such hands as subject to execution.[4] The decision that water works when in the hands of municipal corporations are not subject to execution is, therefore, really not necessary to protect the interests of the people served by them. For just as in the case of their ownership by private companies, it might be recognized that they might be sold on execution, subject, of course, to the condition that when in the hands of the vendee on such sale the service of distributing water to the public should be uninterrupted. Other cases, not so directly in point, but still discussing this matter, and decided largely as a result of the application of these principles, are Davenport v. The Peoria Insurance

60 Missouri, 23; President, etc., v. Indianapolis, 12 Indiana, 620. See also Lowe v. Board, 94 Indiana, 553.

[1] See Fleishel v. Hightower, 62 Georgia, 324.
[2] New Orleans v. Morris, 105 U. S. 600.
[3] Foster v. Fowler, 60 Penn. St. 27.
[4] Guest v. Merion Water Co., 142 Penn. St. 610.

Company,[1] in which it is held that, where a statute provided that the public buildings or property " necessary and proper for the carrying out of the general purposes " for which the city was incorporated were to be exempt from execution, judgments against the city were not incumbrances so as to void a policy of insurance upon the city hospital when such policy was issued on the condition that there were no incumbrances on the property ; and Schaffer *v.* Cadwallader,[2] where it was held that a judgment against a municipal corporation was not a lien upon its real estate in the absence of statute. In this latter case the land in question had been used for a city hospital and a city street, but was later conveyed by the city to a private individual, and at the time of the conveyance judgments existed against the city. It was decided that such judgments were not incumbrances on the title so as to violate the provisions of a contract to sell the property free from incumbrances. In the case of Birmingham *v.* Rumsey,[3] it is said that execution may issue against the private property not useful or used for corporate purposes precisely as against the property of individuals ; and in Louisville *v.* The Commonwealth,[4] it is held that as a result of statute the private

[1] 17 Iowa, 276.
[2] 36 Penn. St. 126.
[3] 63 Alabama, 352.
[4] 1 Duval, Kentucky, 295.

property of the city, that is, property not used for carrying on its municipal government but only for the convenience or profit of its citizens collectively which it owns as a private corporation, is subject to taxation. In this case, it is intimated that water works are private property and are subject to taxation in the hands of the municipality. Such are some of the important cases holding what is public property from the point of view of what municipal property may be sold on execution. On the other hand, it has been held that the seizure by execution and garnishment process of amounts due the city from street railway companies as a *bonus* for privileges granted, and from certain warehouse companies as a lease of sugar-shed warehouses, was perfectly proper, inasmuch as this was private property and under the statute subject to execution;[1] also, that execution may issue against city property consisting of the bonds of a water-works company and a railway company;[2] and against a bond in favour of a municipality received from a private person in satisfaction of a judgment against him for expenses for sidewalks in front of his property.[3] It has been held also,

---

[1] Hart v. New Orleans, 12 Fed. Rep. 292.

[2] New Orleans v. Home Mutual Insurance Co., 23 La. Ann. 61.

[3] Municipality No. 3 v. Hart, 6 La. Ann. 507.

that certain property called "beach and water-lot property," which had been granted to the city of San Francisco by the legislature, could be sold on execution of a judgment against the city. The case came up in the following way: The defendant Frisbie, in an action of ejectment brought against him by one claiming title to the land under a conveyance of a board of land commissioners, based his title, among other things, on the sheriff's deed given as a result of a sale in execution of a judgment, and the court upheld his title, notwithstanding the fact of a proviso in the original grant to the city that the city should pay into the state treasury within twenty-five days after the receipt twenty-five per cent of all moneys arising from the sale of the property. It was held that this proviso was not a condition annexed to the grant, for the non-performance of which the estate of the city could be defeated, nor did it create a trust in favour of the state so far as the property itself was concerned. The court said, the interest of the city in the property "is absolute, qualified by no conditions, and subject to no specific uses. It is therefore a leviable interest subject to sale under execution, and such interest in the premises in controversy passed to the defendant upon sale and conveyance under his judgment in execution." [1]

[1] Holladay v. Frisbie, 15 California, 630.

Finally, a market bazar in which eatables are not sold, and which is therefore not regarded as a public market, may, if rented by a municipal corporation, which thus derives a revenue from it, be sold on execution.[1]

The contradictory views expressed by the courts as to the public or private character of water works and other such property are explainable by their points of view in the particular decisions. For while the class of property represented by them is so local in character and of such particular advantage to the localities served by them that such localities may with perfect propriety be held to possess inviolable rights of property in them and to be liable for negligence in their management, they do not on that account cease to be public in character in the sense that they subserve a purpose of administration. They are, it is true, local, but they do not therefore cease to be governmental in character. Being governmental in character, the rules of the private law should not be permitted to govern them to the disadvantage of that local public which is benefited by them, even if thereby the rights of private individuals are subserved. For *salus populi suprema est lex.*

[1] New Orleans *v.* Morris, 3 Woods C. C. **103**.

CHAPTER XI

WHAT IS THE SPHERE OF PRIVATE MUNICIPAL ACTION RECOGNIZED BY THE AMERICAN LAW

OUR discussion of the sphere of municipal home rule has, on account of the interesting questions arising in connection with it, it must be confessed, led us at times somewhat far afield, and it becomes necessary on that account to sum up our conclusions as to what by the present American law is recognized as the sphere of private action of municipal corporations.

As has been intimated, the courts have, in their interpretation of the constitutional restrictions of the power of control of the legislature over municipal affairs, considered the prohibition of *special legislation* contained therein as more important than the prohibition to regulate by special legislation *municipal affairs*, and have in many instances given an unduly wide interpretation to the words "municipal" or "local affairs," an interpretation which is not borne out by the decisions in other branches of the law on this point. Further, the decisions as to the property of municipal corporations have been rendered of much less value than they otherwise would have been, and even than in former times they were, on account, on the one hand, of the great desire of the courts to protect the private rights of individuals dealing with municipal corporations, which has resulted in their holding these bodies responsible for neglect in connection with all property, and, on the other hand, by the feeling that the individuals composing municipal corporations should be protected against extravagance on the part of municipal authorities in connection with municipal property, and that the continuous operation of public administrative services should not be interfered with by the forced sale of the property used therefor. If, however, we bear these facts in mind, and consequently do not allow the decisions made as to these particular points too great an influence in the determination of what is the sphere of private action of municipal corporations, we will, perhaps, be justified in concluding somewhat as follows:

Firstly. The geographical foundation, or territorial basis, of the municipal corporation is a matter which is so closely connected with its corporate life, that the legislature may not, under the usual constitutional restrictions of legislative power, interfere with it where this interference takes on the form of special action.

Secondly. The general administrative organization of the municipal corporation in the same way is a matter in which it has special concern, and may not, under the usual constitutional restrictions, be interfered with by special legislative action, while under not a few of the constitutions the legislature is not allowed, even by general laws, to take away from the people of the municipality the right to elect, either directly or indirectly, their own officers. Some of the cases (particularly those of Michigan) go so far as to claim that this right of local election is one guaranteed to the people of the localities by our general system of government, and is therefore one which may not be infringed upon by the legislature, even in the absence of specific constitutional protection. This is, however, an extreme view, and is not believed to be justified by the law as it exists at present. It is, however, to be remembered that, even under the usual constitutional restrictions, the legislature may, for the purpose of attending to some particular branches of administration, organize, by special act, new local areas, as, *e.g.*, police districts, sanitary districts, and drainage districts. This tends very much to weaken the force of all the constitutional provisions protecting municipal rights.

Thirdly. Municipal corporations are, in accordance with general laws, to fix the salaries and determine the duties of their officers, which may not be increased or decreased by the legislature by interfering with the duties or salaries of the officers of specific cities where the usual constitutional restrictions obtain.

Fourthly. It may be regarded as a settled rule of the law, which the courts apply, whatever may be their point of view, that all officers engaged in the exercise and execution of police powers in the broad sense of the word, that is, in preserving the public peace, safety, and health, are not, whether they are under the control of the municipal authorities or not, officers of the corporation, since the corporation, in attending to these matters, is not acting as a local corporation, but as an agent of the government. On the other hand, officers engaged in the performance of duties connected with local public works and improvements, among which may be mentioned primarily sewerage, drainage, and water-works, and by the weight of authority also streets, are local officers; that is, in the performance of duties connected with these matters, the corporation is acting rather as a private or local corporation than a public governmental agency.

Fifthly. In raising money to defray purely local

expenses, — that is, for matters designated "local," in the preceding paragraph, — through the powers either of taxation or of assessment for improvements, the municipality is acting as an organization for the satisfaction of local needs, that is, in a *quasi*-private capacity; and, while it must look to the general statutes for authority, inasmuch as the power of taxation, in which that of local assessment is from this point of view to be included, is a legislative power, it may not, under the usual constitutional restrictions, be interfered with either by the legislature by means of the passage of special acts, or by the courts by means of their power to hold it responsible for negligence. So long as it follows the provisions of the general law, under the usual constitutional restrictions, it is to decide upon the necessity of undertaking these works uncontrolled by special legislative action; and, provided the system which it adopts does not directly encroach upon private rights, it is also the sole uncontrolled judge of the manner in which it shall provide for the satisfaction of the needs which it has determined exist. In so far, however, as it enters into the relations of the private law in carrying out these powers, it is subject, as is any private corporation or individual, to be controlled by the courts, which will see that it follows the law. Thus the courts may, in order to protect private rights, insist that the municipality exercise to the full its financial and particularly its taxing powers, so far as this may be necessary to the fulfilment of its obligations, may prevent it from acting contrary to the provisions of law, and may hold it liable for negligence in carrying out the plans of public improvements which it has determined upon as well as in maintaining such completed works in proper condition.

Sixthly. The courts agree in holding that property held by a municipal corporation, which is used primarily for the purposes of revenue, and is not used specifically and definitely for any of its governmental or administrative purposes, is private in character, and is therefore to be governed by the rules of the private law. Thus the legislature may not deprive a city of such property except as it may deprive a private person, that is, either with its consent or upon giving it compensation. Here it must be admitted that some of the cases go further than the logic of the law requires in insuring their property rights to municipalities, recognizing not only that private municipal property is in the same manner as the property of individuals protected by constitutional provisions protecting private property, but also that the same protection is to be accorded to property held by the city for public purposes. The question whether the legislature may exercise a control over the strictly private property, that is, the property of the first class mentioned, cannot be regarded as settled, though several cases in the lower courts claim for such property an immunity from legislative control, so long as the corporation remains in existence. Where judgments against municipalities may be collected by execution, which is regarded as the better common-law rule, it is held that execution may issue against claims and debts due the city and against property such as lands or bonds and stock owned by the city and not used for administrative or public purposes, but not against money obtained from taxes, nor against claims for unpaid taxes, nor against public buildings owned by the city and the furniture contained within them, nor against property dedicated to a public use or affected by a public trust. The public character of such property still remains, notwithstanding changes in its form, as, for example, where a public building has been burned, the insurance money due or paid is exempt from execution. Finally, as a result of the power to act as a subject of private law, corporations may alien either absolutely or conditionally, that is, mortgage, the same property that is subject to execution, and only such property.

Seventhly. As a further result of their position

as subjects of private law, municipal corporations may make contracts upon which they are liable, as are ordinary corporations and individuals, and may, like individuals, be guilty of tort so far as the act or omission by which the damage complained of is caused is an act or omission within the realm of the private law, that is, is not connected with their legislative or police powers, as above defined. Their torts can, however, as a matter of fact, be committed almost alone in connection with their management of property. By the later decisions, further, the purpose for which property under their control is used is not allowed to have any effect on their liability, though the older decisions claimed for municipalities the same immunity from liability as is granted the state when they are managing property used for administrative or governmental purposes. Municipal corporations may, it is true, theoretically be guilty of tort unconnected with the management of property and the exercise of governmental powers in about the same way as may ordinary individuals, but in the nature of things this seldom happens. Streets may from this point of view be regarded as property without doing great violence to the subject, and are so regarded by one of the latest authors writing upon the subject of municipal liability.[1]

[1] Jones, *Negligence of Municipal Corporations*, p. 110.

The later constitutions are attempting more and more to protect the rights of municipalities to control the streets against encroachment on the part of the legislature, thus recognizing in them certain rights very analogous to those of property. In so far, however, as streets are not regarded as property, the liability of municipalities for their proper care is to be regarded as arising out of the negligence of the performance of a duty imposed upon them for their local and private advantage, and as an exception to the rule that the torts which they may commit are always in connection with property.

The result is, that the sphere of home rule or local, private action assigned to municipal corporations by the American law, may be said to include merely the powers to undertake and maintain public works of peculiar interest to them, and to acquire and hold property both for the purposes of such public works and for the general purposes of revenue. In acting thus as local and *quasi*-private corporations, they are subjects of the private law, and as such enjoy, as a result of general constitutional provisions protecting private property, almost the same exemption from legislative control over their property as is enjoyed by individuals and private corporations. But the narrow meaning assigned by the courts to the term "special act" has lessened very greatly the protection which the special constitutional provisions in regard to municipal autonomy attempted to insure to them. While their property is comparatively safe from legislative interference, their rights of decision and action in this sphere of private legal relations are still subject to be interfered with by the legislature, notwithstanding the fact they are held up to almost all the liabilities of private persons for their actions in this sphere, and are by the better rule of the common law liable to have private claims against them enforced by resort to their property not used for administrative purposes which they may also alien. So far as they act outside of this sphere they act as government, are in this respect subjects not of the private but of the public law, are therefore under the control of the legislature and not liable for their actions not in the nature of a contract and not connected with the care of property any more than is the government.

While such is the sphere of private and local action of municipal corporations, which is derived from a consideration of the entire law relative to these bodies, it is to be remembered it is not the sphere in which, in the absence of special constitutional provisions assuring to them the right of local autonomy, they may move free from legislative control. Aside from the general constitutional provisions protecting property, which apply to municipal property as well as to the property of individuals, and aside from a few decisions mostly confined to one commonwealth, viz., that of Michigan, which claim that this sphere of local autonomy is assured to municipal corporations by our general system of government, municipal corporations are, in the absence of the special constitutional provisions referred to protecting the right to local autonomy, at the mercy of the legislature. For they are subjects of the public law, of which the legislature is the constitutional expounder. Further, the narrow material and financial powers recognized as belonging to municipal corporations necessarily circumscribe quite closely their sphere of action. Care should be taken, therefore, not to assume, because municipal corporations are held, from the standpoint of their obligations and property rights of a private legal character, to be in a *quasi*-private position, that they are on that account either free to act without special authorization, or are, in the absence of specific constitutional provisions to that effect, independent of legislative regulation and control. Not only does the legislature, when not prohibited by the constitution, habitually interfere in local affairs, but the constitutional provisions which attempt to take away its powers in this respect have been so narrowly construed by the courts that they have had comparatively little effect in remedying the evils they were passed to obviate.

CHAPTER XII

EUROPEAN METHODS OF DISTINGUISHING AND SECURING THE SPHERE OF MUNICIPAL HOME RULE

Enough, it is believed, has been said in the preceding pages both to show that the American legislature has very commonly interfered in the purely local affairs of municipalities, and to prove as well that this interference has been productive of great evil. It is believed that it has been shown also that this interference on the part of the legislature has been due to its failure, excusable for the reasons that have been pointed out, and perfectly natural, from the historical point of view, to distinguish a sphere of local municipal action among the many duties which have been imposed upon the municipality by the American law, and that the attempts to stop such legislative interference by constitutional restriction of the power of special legislation have very largely failed. The question now presents itself whether it is possible to distinguish a sphere of action in which a municipality should be allowed the same freedom as is granted to a private corporation; whether a municipality can be assigned a sphere of municipal home rule, and at the same time the necessary central control over matters of general interest can be assured. A consideration of modern English and continental arrangements may aid us in answering this question. Modern English local government dates from the Poor-Law Amendment Act of 1834. Previous to that time the English local government system was similar to our present American system, in the fact that the central government made as much use as possible of local officers practically independent of all central administrative control for the transaction of business which primarily interested the state as a whole. Among the many matters thus attended to by local officers and paid for by the local taxpayers was the subject of public charity, which was organized and administered under the provisions of the great Poor Law of Elizabeth. The exercise of these powers by local officers, uncontrolled by any central administrative authority, resulted in a complete lack of uniformity in methods, and great extravagance and inefficiency. Each locality, further, moved by its own selfish ends, administered the law in such a way that its interests alone were considered, and the interests of the state as a whole and society in general were almost completely disregarded. The remedy for these evils was found in a resumption by the central government of the powers which it had abdicated.

The Poor-Law Amendment Act of 1834, which was passed as a result of the report of the Poor-Law Commission of 1833, and which was intended to remedy the evils that had been produced by the formerly uncontrolled local administration of public charity, provided for a system of central administrative control over the administration of this most important branch of public activity. This law did, it is true, provide for a local poor-law authority, whose members were to be elected by the persons whose pockets were affected by the administration of the law, that is, the local ratepayers, but it subjected the actions of this local authority to the control of a central poor-law board which received power to prevent local extravagance in the administration of the law, and to secure harmony and uniformity in its administration throughout the entire country.

The lesson which England learned from its experience with the uncontrolled local administration of an important branch of government, affecting the state as a whole, was never forgotten. The reorganization of the various branches of administration which has gone on during this century has been made upon the lines of the Poor-Law Amendment Act of 1834. When England began to regard the care of the public health as a branch of public administration, it provided an organization which ran through the cities, as well as the rural districts, very similar to that provided for the administration of the poor law by the Poor-Law Amendment Act of 1834. In the various districts which were formed for the administration of the public health were placed bodies, elected, it is true, by the local ratepayers, but, like the boards of poor-law guardians, subjected to a most detailed and efficient central control, to be exercised by an administrative body at London, the Public Health Board.

When, again, in 1870, the government began to regard the matter of education as one of its proper branches of administration, it followed the same plan. The country was divided into school districts, and in each one of the school districts where public schools were necessary was placed a body, elected by the taxpayers of the community, but subjected at the same time to the control of the new department of education, now known as the Committee of the Privy Council on Education. Both of the existing central authorities — namely, the Local Government Board, which was formed in 1871, as a result of the consolidation of the old central Poor-Law Board and the Public Health Board, and the Committee of the Council on Education — have most extended powers of control over the various local authorities, which are entrusted with the exercise of powers in these various administrative branches. The Local Government Board has the right to veto all appointments to office by the boards of poor-law guardians, and without its consent none of the officers of these bodies may be removed from office. It also has the right to issue general orders controlling the general conduct of the boards of poor-law guardians, and to send out inspectors and auditors, who are to see that the provisions of the law and the rules of the Local Government Board are observed; and who also have the right to refuse their approval, which is necessary to the validity of the action of the local boards, to all expenditures which have been made contrary to the provisions of either the Poor-Law Amendment Act or the rules of the Local Government Board. Since 1871, when the Local Government Board became as well the central sanitary authority, it has had an important control over the administration of the public health. In case of the refusal of the local health authorities to do what the Local Government Board considers to be necessary for the preservation of the public health, it has the right to appoint a temporary commission to do what is necessary, and to raise the money expended by such commission by means of a rate, to be levied on the ratepayers of the locality. Practically the same powers with reference to education are granted to the Education Department. If this body finds, as a result of an investigation, that there is not sufficient accommodation for the children of a given locality in the private schools which come up to the government requirements, it has the right to order the election of a school board in the district, which then may levy taxes and borrow money for the support of the public schools, or board schools, as they are called, which are established by such school boards. If the locality refuses to proceed to such an election, the Education Department has the right to proceed as the Local Government Board has in the case of bad sanitary conditions. It also distributes to the schools coming up to the government's standard, which fact is determined by its inspectors, the pecuniary aid given by Parliament. Further, with the exception of the sanitary administration, where the general local authorities in the urban districts — as, for example, the borough councils in the boroughs, and the district councils in the urban county districts — are the sanitary authorities, the new legislation has formed special authorities for the purpose of administering the various laws of general concern in the localities. It has not granted to the ordinary local authorities, such as the parish authorities and the county or city corporations, the power to administer these various branches. Thus, in the poor-law administration, we have a special authority in the board of poor-law guardians; and in the education administration, we have a special school board, which, even in the municipal boroughs — which are, as well, school districts — is unconnected in any way with the other local authorities in the districts. The larger and more populous boroughs have, indeed, charge of the police. This is, however, due to the fact that, historically, the care of the police has always been regarded, in accordance with the principles of the original scheme of local self-government, as a matter which the larger boroughs, at any rate, should have in their own control. The administration of the police is, nevertheless, regarded at the present time as a matter which concerns the interests of the state as a whole. This is seen from the method adopted to provide for a central control over this branch of administration. An act of 1856 practically provided for a consolidation of the police in all boroughs with a population under 5000 with the general police of the country, which was managed by the county authorities. The new Local Government Act of 1888 provided also for a consolidation with the county police force, of the police force of all boroughs, with a population under 10,000. The police force, also, in the various urban county districts, which are embryonic municipal organizations, is not managed by the district authority, but by the authority which manages the general police of the country, namely, the county authorities. It was not considered advisable at the time of the reorganization of the municipalities by the Consolidated Municipal Corporations Act of 1882, or at the time of the passage of the Local Government Act of 1888, to go further in this direction of bringing the police under direct central administration. At the same time, however, a scheme has been devised, which practically has resulted in a very large measure of central control over the police, even in the largest boroughs. The act of 1856, to which reference has already been made, provided that the Secretary of State might grant a certificate that the police in all the local districts were kept up to a certain state of efficiency; and, in case such certificate was granted, that the treasury should pay a share of the expenses of their pay and clothing. In this manner, the central government has a most important means of controlling the administration of the police in all of the localities.

It will be seen, thus, that the state either has formed special authorities under the direct control of a central administrative authority for the administration of matters which concern the state as a whole rather than the locality, or has, where it has permitted any of the local corporations authority with regard to matters of central concern, subjected the exercise of the powers granted to a central administrative control. While in the case of the police of the larger boroughs this central control is an indirect one, and is not necessarily exercised, as the boroughs may renounce all claim to the grant in aid, in the case of the public health it is direct. For in the management of the public health, all of the various local authorities which have large sanitary powers, such as borough councils, are subjected to the same control as are the local authorities which have been formed merely for the purpose of attending to this one branch of administration.

At the same time, however, that England has been thus centralizing all branches of administration which are of interest to the state at large, it has been granting to the various local corporations, such as the boroughs, counties, and parishes, more and more power with regard to their purely local matters, and has devised a method of granting such local powers which has not only reduced the danger of central legislative regulation of local affairs to a minimum, but has also completely obviated the probability — it might almost be said the possibility — of the sacrifice of local institutions at the altar of national politics. That there was danger in granting independent local authorities uncontrolled powers over the discharge of central functions was not the only lesson England learned from her experience previous to 1835. It was also learned that efficiency and uprightness in local government might be, and indeed had been, in English municipal history sacrificed in the interest of partisan politics ; and it was also believed that the most easy way of ensuring such sacrifice was the incorporation of municipalities by special act. Just so soon as the narrow self-electing municipal council had been developed out of the broad and democratic municipal organization originally to be found in England, this narrow council was seized upon first by the Crown and afterwards by the nobles, as a means of increasing their influence in Parliament, many of whose members were elected by the city corporations. This was done first by the Tudors to further the interests of the great religious reformation which they had so much at heart, afterwards by the Stuarts in their struggles with the constitutional party, and finally, by the nobles after the revolution of 1688 both in their struggles with the Crown, and with each other as represented in the great political parties of the eighteenth and early part of the nineteenth centuries. From the time that it was seen that municipal corporations could be used as pawns in the game of national politics they lost both their importance as administrative institutions, and almost all their powers of local self-government. All sorts of influences were brought to bear to deprive them of their character as representatives of the municipal population. All new charters that were granted formed close corporations, usually with self-electing governing bodies, which could easily be controlled by the national political parties; and the courts were induced both to legitimize usurpations by such narrow bodies on the right of the municipal populations to choose their rulers,[1] and to permit themselves to be used by the Crown in the crusade against municipal liberties undertaken by it through the issue of the *quo warranto* in the later part of the Stuart period. In a great number of cases liberal municipal charters were in this way forfeited, and many corporations, alarmed by these actions, surrendered

---

[1] They held that any custom which provided for the narrow self-electing town council was valid even if contrary to the charter. See the case of corporations decided in the reign of Elizabeth, Dillon, *op. cit.*, Vol. I., p. 18; and Ireland *v.* Free Borough, 12 Co. 120.

their charters. In all cases new and less liberal charters were granted.¹ This was the second lesson that England learned, and this also has not been forgotten. It was seen that under the system of special charters municipal government had been sacrificed to national politics, and that as a result, purely municipal affairs had been so inefficiently administered that even the corrupt Parliaments of the eighteenth century had not thought proper to entrust municipal corporations with many even purely local functions.² The commission which was appointed to investigate the municipal corporations reported in favour of a general municipal corporation act which was passed in 1835. The purposes of the act were to provide a general scheme of municipal organization which was to be introduced into all cities except London, and to revive interest in local matters by the grant to municipal corporations of large powers of local government.

The municipal corporations act, in the first place, gave to the borough council almost complete power to determine the municipal organization, providing that the council should, from time to time, appoint such officers in the borough as

---

¹ See Dillon, *op. cit.*, Vol. I, p. 18; Rex. *v.* London, 8 How. St. Tr. 1039, 1340 ; Allinson & Penrse, Philadelphia, p. 10.

² *Supra*, p. 14.

it might think necessary, and might, at any time, discontinue the appointment of any officer appearing to them not necessary to be reappointed. In the second place, it provided for a transfer to the borough council of the powers of the various special authorities which had been established, on account of the incapacity of the corporate authorities under the old organization, to provide for matters of particular local importance. It was provided, also, that in case the revenue from the property of the corporation were insufficient for the expenditures of the borough, the borough council should have the power to levy a borough rate. The borough was also permitted to borrow money for specific purposes, but its borrowing powers were subjected to the approval of some central authority, either the Local Government Board or the Treasury Department. Since the passage of the Municipal Corporations Act of 1835, very many other powers have been conferred by general act upon municipal corporations. Such are, for example, the labouring classes' lodging-houses' act and the artisan and labourers' dwellings' act, which permit the various municipal corporations to provide for the housing of the working classes. Such are also the acts relating to public libraries, or museums, or schools for science and art, which permit the municipal corporations to provide these means of instruction and amusement for their population. Such, also, are the tramways acts and the various acts relating to municipal water works and gas works, which permit the municipal corporations, under certain conditions, either to acquire these properties when in the hands of private persons, or, where they have not been organized within the municipal corporation, to organize these various services, either under the direct management of the municipal corporations or else, although owned by the municipal corporations, to be operated by some private company. A good description of the progress which English municipal corporations have made in this direction is to be found in the excellent work recently published by Mr. Albert Shaw on "Municipal Government in Great Britain." What was done for the municipal boroughs by the Municipal Corporations Act of 1835, has also been done for other thickly populated sections which have not obtained the full organization of the municipal boroughs, and which were called until last year either local government districts or urban sanitary districts, but which are now dignified by the name of urban county districts. The first step in this direction was made by the public health act which was, with its amendments, finally consolidated in 1875. Numerous other statutes have extended the powers of these local governmental organizations, and the new local government act of 1894 has not only increased their efficiency and powers, but has, at the same time, attempted to provide for the parish itself a municipal corporate organization, and has granted to it very much larger powers than were theretofore possessed by this historic area of the English local governmental system. One thing, however, is to be noticed in connection with this increase of the local powers of these various bodies. Not only has the legislation of the nineteenth century pretty clearly distinguished between local affairs and affairs of central importance, which have been kept pretty closely under central administrative control, if they have not been put into the hands of special authorities, organized for this purpose, and directly under the supervision of some central administrative authority; but in order to prevent the exercise of the purely local powers which have been granted to the various local corporations from resulting in the assumption of too great financial burdens, it has provided for a strong administrative control, to be exercised by the central authorities in London, over the action of the local authorities, so far as that action will result in the exercise of particularly the borrowing power, and in many instances also the taxing power. The consent of the Local Government Board at London is generally required in order that loans may be issued, and very strict provisions have been passed as to the amount of money which may be borrowed, which is generally a proportion of the ratable value of the property assessed for the purposes of local taxation, and also as to the time for which such money may be borrowed and as to the necessary sinking fund to be provided for its payment.

It will be seen from this slight sketch of the local government legislation of the nineteenth century, how far England has departed from the original idea of English local self-government. While we in America have carried the original idea much further than it was ever attempted to carry it in England, while we have regarded the city, as well as the town and the county, as an agent of public administration, and have conferred upon the city functions of central government, with the result of the failure of the legislature to distinguish between purely central and purely local functions, and of the extension of the control which it should have over the central functions of government to the functions of purely local government; England has made a pretty clear distinction between central and local affairs, has subjected the central affairs to a strong central control, which, however, has very largely changed in character, has become administrative rather than legislative, and has, at the same time, conferred upon the local corporations a very large measure of local autonomy. But even as to such purely local powers, the English legislation of the nineteenth century has seen fit to provide a central control, so far as the exercise of these powers will result in the assumption by the localities of financial burdens. This control is, however, as in the case of the control over the purely central functions of government, an administrative one, for the most part. It is not meant, by this statement, to say that the former legislative control, by means of special and local acts, has been formally done away with, or is never, at the present time, exercised. But the mere fact that the general organization and powers of municipal corporations have, since 1835, been, for the most part, regulated by general acts has, of necessity, relieved the legislature from a great temptation. A great temptation to legislative interference has been removed also by the grant to these local corporations of the power themselves to organize their own detailed administrative system. The legal omnipotence of the English Parliament has been, however, in no way interfered with, because such a thing as constitutional restriction of legislative power is unknown to the English system. At the same time, the framers of the English municipal institutions of the nineteenth century have been thoroughly convinced of the inadvisability of attempting to regulate local matters by means of the action of a central legislature. They have hedged about the passage of special legislation with so many formalities, and have required that special legislation shall conform, in so many particulars, to certain general acts which are known as "Clauses Acts," that special legislation has become more general in character, that is, each special act will resemble very largely all other special acts. Special legislation consists merely in the application to specific localities of certain general principles which have been incorporated in certain general acts. It has, at the same time, become so difficult of adoption that it is not nearly so common as it is in this country. Finally, inasmuch as one of the formalities often required is that a special act shall, before it may be passed, be approved by some central administrative authority, this special legislative control is itself subject to an administrative control.[1]

The result is, that at the present time in Eng-

---

[1] For a description of the formalities which are required in the case of special legislation, see De Franqueville, *Le Gouvernement et le Parlement Brittaniques*, Vol. III., Chap. 38.

land, partly owing to the establishment of special organs for the administration of matters of general interest, and partly owing to the substitution of a central administrative for a central legislative control over the affairs of the local bodies whose powers are determined by general acts, a sphere of municipal local autonomy is much more clearly distinguished than here.

In England, this distinction of a sphere of municipal local autonomy has been accomplished through the abandonment of certain of her historic principles of local self-government. On the continent the same distinction has been made, as the result of a development of principles which have always obtained there. While in England the original system of local self-government, as has been shown, consisted in the administration, by administratively independent local authorities, in accordance with the general rules laid down by a central legislature, of all matters of government, of whatever character they might be, whether general or local ; on the continent, the origin of local self-government is to be found in the old feudal idea, which was always stronger upon the continent than in England, of the autonomous rights of the various local communities or corporations.[1]

[1] See Stengel, *Organization der Preussischen Verwaltung*, p. 18. Cf. also Vauthier, *Le Gouvernement Local de l'Angleterre*, 1895, on

These local corporations indeed lost most of their powers, both in France and in Germany, as a result of the centralization of the administration, which was accomplished in the seventeenth and eighteenth centuries; but when, after the French Revolution, the idea of local self-government began again to have an influence, there were very generally incorporated into the municipal corporations acts which were then adopted, and also into those which have been adopted since, two most important principles, one of which certainly has its origin in the old idea of feudal local autonomy. This was the principle, that municipal corporations were to have a sphere of action in which they were to act largely free from all central control. It finds its expression in the clause which is usually contained in the municipal corporations acts granting to the city council the authority to decide as to municipal affairs.[1] The student of American municipal corporations is at once struck, upon his perusal of these continental municipal corporations acts, with the complete absence of any enumera-

---

p. 162, where he compares the English borough with the continental commune.

[1] For an example of the Prussian municipal corporations acts, see Städte, *Ordnung der Provinz Westphalen*, March 19, 1856, sec. 35. See also French Communes Act, April 5, 1884, sec. 68; Loening, *Deutsches Verwaltungsrecht*, p. 169; Leidig, *Preussiches Stadtrecht*, p. 101; Boeuf, *Droit Administratif*, 1884, p. 265.

tion of municipal powers; and until he understands the meaning of the phrase, "the council shall govern by its decisions the affairs of the city," he is apt to believe, on account of the many instances where central approval of some sort is required in order that the action of municipal corporations may be valid, that the sphere of free action of the continental municipal corporation is a very narrow one. But so soon as he understands that this phrase means that the presumption is always in favour of the competence of municipal corporations, and that the central administration has power relative to municipal corporations only where such power has been expressly granted, he perceives that the system adopted for permitting municipal corporations to participate in the work of government is exactly the reverse of that which is adopted in the American and the original English system; and that unless the central administrative control is very great, the continental corporations have really under it greater local powers than are possessed by American municipal corporations. While our method is one of enumerated powers, the continental method is one of general grant of power, subject to specific enumerated restrictions. The municipal corporation may do anything where power has not been conferred specifically upon some other authority, and is subjected to a cen tral control only where the law specifically and expressly provides for such a control. This principle seems to have been first adopted in the Prussian municipal corporations act of 1808, which was due to Baron Stein, and was indeed one of the essential portions of his great administrative reform of the early part of this century. It has been incorporated in most of the other Prussian municipal corporations acts adopted since that time, and has finally been adopted in France in the Communes Act of 1884.

The other characteristic of the continental municipal legislation of this century is that it is general and not special in character. This solution of this most important problem was reached in France quite a time before the Revolution. It was the result of the desire of the absolute monarchy to have a uniform system of municipal administration throughout the country, and was, at first, a means rather of securing an extreme administrative centralization than of providing for municipal home rule.[1] The principle was later

---

[1] See Dareste de la Chavanne, *Histoire de l'Administration en France*, Vol. I., Chap. VI., and particularly page 208, where it is said: "Le but de ces ordonnances [générales] fut d'assurer une part plus considérable à l'influence royale dans le choix des officiers municipaux, de régler les actes de ces officiers sur des principes fixes, enfin de leur enlever toutes les attributions qui convenaient mieux aux agents du pouvoir central."

adopted in Prussia, under the administrative centralization of Frederick William I. and Frederick the Great, and its purpose there was the same as in France.[1] The effect, however, of this method of regulating municipal affairs has been, in this century, to develop municipal local autonomy. The decentralization of the administrative organization which has everywhere been the rule, has prevented the central administration from interfering as much as formerly in municipal affairs, and the principle of general municipal corporation acts, which was adopted when the administrative centralization was greater, prevents the legislature from regulating by special act municipal affairs, or, at any rate, removes it from temptation. It is true that the constitutional system on the continent, on account of there being as in England no efficient constitutional restriction of legislative power, does not legally preclude the legislature from regulating by special act municipal affairs. But, as a matter of fact, the legislature has not made the attempt. One reason why it has not done so is to be found in the fact that the administrative control, provided by the general municipal corporation acts, has made such action unnecessary. The great centralization of administration, which was reached in the eighteenth

[1] See Leidig, *Preussisches Stadtrecht*, pp. 15 *et seq.*

century, brought with it a very important central administrative control. The presence of the central administrative control, which is considerable even now, and which has been exercised from the beginning as well over municipal bodies as other administrative authorities, has made unnecessary special legislative action with regard to municipal affairs. This central administrative control is exercised, not only as in England, over the financial administration of the various municipal corporations, and over those matters of a general character which the corporation is attending to, but also is exercised over the general municipal organization. In both France and Prussia the central administration has the power to dissolve the municipal councils.[1] In Prussia, further, its approval of the appointment by the municipal council of the most important executive officers is necessary. In France it consists also in the power the central government has to dismiss the mayor of a commune from office.[2] But over the purely local matters of the municipal corporation, that is, over the establishment and maintenance of institutions which are of interest alone to its inhabitants, this administrative control does not

---

[1] Bœuf, *op. cit.*, p. 262; Leidig, *op. cit.*, p. 108.

[2] For a description of this central administrative control, see Leidig, *op. cit.*, pp. 48 *et seq.*; Bœuf, *op. cit.*, p. 266.

usually extend, except in so far as the approval of the central administration is necessary to the exercise of financial powers. In Prussia, however, the city executive, which is largely under the control of the central administration, has practically a veto power over even the local acts of the council.

On the continent the provision of special organs for the management of matters affecting the state as a whole is not so common as in England. Thus, in Prussia, the care of education and public sanitation is largely in the hands of the municipal council. The same is true of the public health in France as to its financial side. In both countries the police, also, is under the charge of the municipal corporations, but here, as in the other cases, the control exercised by the central administration is a very strict one, and in Prussia provision is made for the assumption by the central government of the care of the police in most of the larger cities.

It will be seen thus that it is possible to devise a system of municipal government in which matters of purely local concern will not be regulated by the central legislature of the state. It will also be seen that it is possible to do this without providing special organs, apart from the municipal authorities, for the administration of those matters which are not purely local in character, but inter-

s

est as well the state as a whole, although the provision of such special organs for these branches does undoubtedly render the distinction of local from central administrative matters much easier. The English method of providing such special authorities is therefore not absolutely necessary, but in all the three countries it will be seen that the absence of special legislation with regard to municipal corporations is found in connection with general municipal corporations acts and a central administrative control. This control does not usually extend over the exercise of purely local powers, except in so far as these are connected with the most important financial powers. The absence of special legislative regulation of municipal affairs is also always accompanied by the grant of large local powers to the municipal corporations. This is also unavoidable, for these matters must be regulated in some way. If they are not regulated by the municipal corporations as a result of a grant to them either of general powers of local government, or of powers over special matters of local government by general acts, they must be regulated by the central legislature by means of special legislation and *vice versa*. The functions to be discharged by municipal corporations are so important that some provision must be made for their regulation.

In the United States, however, we have chosen, as has been pointed out, a different method of determining the position of our municipal corporations in their relation to the central government of the state. We have not profited by the experience of foreign countries in this respect, partly because that experience has been so recent that our attention has not as yet been directed to it, partly because continental administration, and modern English administration for that matter too, has been based on principles with which not only we are unfamiliar, but which also are, as a matter of fact, quite at variance with our historic political and constitutional principles. The American system of administration, outside of the Federal system, has been until very recently, and to a great extent is, even now, characterized by a lack of concentration. It contains no general hierarchy of superior and inferior officers, and the administrative control which is so characteristic of European administration is conspicuous here only by its almost complete absence. With such an administrative system the frequent action of the legislature in administrative matters is a necessity. For it is the only governmental organ through whose action the imperious needs of administrative harmony in matters of general concern may be satisfied. If this central control is to be abolished some other control must be substituted for it. But on account, perhaps, of the fear of anything which savours of monarchy and centralization, we have, until comparatively recently, refused to grant any administrative control over municipalities, and indeed over administrative matters generally, to the central executive officers of the states. We have indeed, on the contrary, actually lessened the original powers of administrative control and supervision possessed by the governors. This has been done in the face of the fact that our Federal administration, which is the most efficient part of our entire administrative system, has been centralized in the highest degree, and in face of the further fact that in our latest municipal charters the almost universal tendency is towards increasing the administrative control of the mayor over the entire municipal administration. Not only have we refused to provide for an administrative control of the central commonwealth government over the municipalities, as England has done, we have also attempted to destroy the legislative control, in the hope that with that gone our cities would obtain the freedom necessary for their good government and healthy development. Unmindful of the dangers of uncontrolled local management of general and even of municipal affairs, and regardless of the public position of most of cities, we have attempted to protect municipal rights, and particularly the supposed right of local autonomy, in somewhat the same manner as we had theretofore protected private rights generally. We have forbidden the legislature to take any special, and, in some cases, even general, action with regard to municipal affairs. This practically amounts to the destruction of the central legislative control over the localities. That we have not suffered from the dangers which are to be apprehended from such a course has been due altogether to the action of the courts when called upon to construe the constitutional provisions prohibiting such special legislative action. There is a close analogy between the position of the courts relative to these constitutional provisions protecting the rights of local government of municipalities and their position relative to the general constitutional provisions protecting the private rights of individuals. In the latter case they have been forced, by the exaggerated extent which they at first assigned to these private rights, to adopt an equally exaggerated idea of the extent of the police power,[1] which it is held is not limited by the constitutional provisions protecting private rights,[2] an idea whose application has threatened the very existence of

---

[1] Cf. Burgess, *Political Science*, etc., Vol. I., p. 214.
[2] *Supra*, p. 38.

private rights.[1] In the former case, like the legislature, the courts have been unable to distinguish private municipal rights from public governmental functions interesting the state as a whole, although, unlike the legislature which has allowed itself to regulate local matters on the ground they were of public concern, the courts have permitted themselves to include within the term "municipal affairs" many matters really public in character, and interesting the whole community.[2] This is due very largely to historical reasons which have always, owing to the conservatism of the courts, had great influence with them. For our system of government has, from an early period, made use of local corporations for the discharge of central administrative functions. Nothing was therefore more easy than to confound the character of governmental functions with the character of the bodies which had been historically called upon to discharge them. The fact that they have thus assigned an unduly wide extent to the sphere of municipal liberty, which was to be protected by the constitutional provisions restricting the power of the legislature to interfere by special

---

[1] It must be admitted that of late, in certain of the cases relative to the constitutionality of acts regulating railway rates, they have somewhat receded from their most advanced position. See Reagan v. Farmers' Loan and Trust Co., 154 U. S. 362.

[2] See Supra, p. 77.

act in this sphere, has obliged the courts to give an unduly narrow meaning to the term "special act" if they were to preserve in an at all efficient condition the only central control over local corporations existing in our system. This action on their part has, however, rendered most of these constitutional provisions almost valueless as a means of protecting the real local-governmental rights of local corporations. For, as has been shown, after as well as before the adoption of these constitutional provisions the legislature has had the power to pass acts relative to municipal affairs which affect only a single local corporation, provided that such acts are so framed as to apply in the future to other corporations which may, by the growth of population, come within their application. The conviction of the failure of this method of preventing special legislative action relative to municipal affairs has, undoubtedly, caused the limitation of the number of classes of cities which has been inserted in some of the later state constitutions, notably in those of Kentucky and New York, which, as has been shown, even define in detail the classes of cities in the state.

At the same time that local rights and central governmental functions have been thus confused by both the legislature and the courts when the question was considered from the point of view of the public law, *i.e.* from that of central control over local corporations, a clear distinction between these two classes of municipal functions has been reached when the question was viewed from the point of view of the private law, *i.e.* from that of the inviolability and alienability of private municipal property, and particularly from that of the liability for tort of municipal corporations.

Why is it that what is quite possible of accomplishment in the one case seems to be impossible in the other? Is it not because the American city is discharging so many functions, interesting directly or indirectly the state at large, that the central government cannot, with due regard to the uniformity of administrative methods in the discharge of such functions and to the general welfare, resign the only central control over them known to our administrative system? Finally, are not the conditions of the various cities within a given state so varied as to make it impossible to govern them all to advantage by one general law, which attempts to fix in their details the municipal organization and the functions which this organization is to discharge? This was evidently the opinion of the late constitutional convention of New York, which, instead of prohibiting special legislation, merely hedged it about with formalities which it was hoped would prevent it from having evil results. These are the reasons, also, why the courts have, through the exercise of their powers of interpretation, almost nullified the constitutional provisions requiring general acts for the incorporation and regulation of municipalities. The fact that they have, when looking at the matter from the private-legal point of view, been able to delimit quite satisfactorily and logically a sphere of municipal private action, would prove beyond a doubt that the failure to accomplish the same result, when considering the matter from the public-legal point of view, was not due to lack of judicial knowledge or powers of legal perception. They have simply refused, in the way so characteristic of courts entrusted with powers of judicial legislation, to apply to conditions, where its application would be fraught with evil, a general legal principle of which they were perfectly well aware, and for whose development in its proper sphere they were themselves responsible.

The fact that they have acted thus has probably saved us both from stagnation in municipal development and disintegration in the administration of central matters. That we have not secured municipal home rule is not their fault, but rather that of a system which, while of great advantage at the time it was formed, has not only outlived its usefulness, but has also been discarded by the country which gave it birth, and from which we inherited it. The old English principle of granting to local authorities, independent of the central administration, general as well as local powers, and subjecting such bodies to a legislative control to be exercised by special and local legislation, has been replaced in England itself by the continental principle of subjecting local authorities discharging functions of central government to a central administrative control, and of allowing local corporations to be formed with large powers of local government, which, where they are to be subject to central control at all, are to be subject to an administrative rather than a legislative control. England has applied to the whole domain of the law of municipal corporations the continental principle of local autonomy, subject in certain cases to central administrative control. In the United States, however, we have applied the local corporate idea merely to the private legal part of that branch of the law. Private-legal liability is accompanied in England as on the continent by local autonomy, and responsibility in and for local matters. In the United States we have merely developed the principle of local liability. The new method adopted in the New York constitution, while preferable to any of the other American methods of preventing the legislative control from becoming legislative regulation of local affairs, and while promising to be efficient in protecting cities against the worst kind of interference in such local affairs, does not insure them the local automony, especially the local initiative, without which local development is difficult if not impossible.[1] It further does not provide a responsible control over those matters over which a central control must be exercised. The old, irresponsible legislative control will continue in the future as in the past.

Greater powers of local government should be granted to the cities, which should also be subjected to a responsible administrative control. Such is the teaching of the experience of the world on this matter. To the objection that changes made in accordance with it would be too radical, it may be answered that they were not too radical for England to make when confronted at the beginning of this century with problems similar to those with which we are now confronted in the United States. Her example should encourage us to follow in her footsteps. For nowhere else, it may be said, is municipal government at the present time more successfully administered, and nowhere else are the tasks it has taken upon itself to perform of greater magnitude.

[1] Witness the relations of the city of New York with the present legislature.

Further, it may be pointed out that a central administrative control is not unknown in the later administrative development of the United States. As a general thing the whole educational administration has been quite highly centralized within the past half century.[1] In New York, also, the administration of the public health by the local authorities is subjected to quite an administrative control and supervision, to be exercised by the State Public Health Board.[2] Within the last few years the whole matter of the care of the pauper lunatics in New York has, with the exception of a few localities, been taken out of the hands of the local authorities, and is now attended to by the central administration of the state which had also previously organized such services as factory inspection and railway supervision under its immediate control. Very generally, also, the uncontrolled exercise of powers of assessment by local authorities has led to such glaring inequalities in the burdens of state taxes, in the case of the apportioned taxes, such as the general property tax, that this whole matter is subjected to a central administrative control to be exercised by a

---

[1] See, e.g., the powers granted to the Superintendent of Public Instruction by the Consolidated School Act of New York, Laws 1864, c. 555, Title 1.

[2] See Laws 1885, c. 270.

state board of assessors or state board of equalization.[1] With that common sense, which, as has already been pointed out, is characteristic of the people of this country, we have, notwithstanding our supposed adhesion to the political theory of local self-government or administration, not hesitated to centralize our administrative system by subjecting our local authorities to a central administrative control, whenever we have seen that uncontrolled local action has led either to administrative inefficiency or inequality of financial burdens. That we are becoming convinced that our historic theory of local government is leading to bad results also in the case of our local municipal corporations, is finally seen from the passage within recent years of laws in various parts of the country requiring a central audit of the accounts of these local corporations. Such laws have been passed in Massachusetts,[2] Minnesota,[3] Mississippi,[4] North Dakota,[5] South Da-

---

[1] The report just made to the legislature of the state of New York by the counsel, appointed by Laws 1892, c. 666, to revise the tax laws, proposes to extend this administrative control to the actions of local assessors in regard to individual assessments, by giving the taxpayer an appeal from the local assessors to a board of State Commissioners of Taxes which it proposes to establish.

[2] Laws 1887, c. 438.

[3] Laws 1878, c. 83; Laws 1891, c. 53; which extended the powers of the "Public Examiner to the city of St. Paul."

[4] Laws 1890, c. 8.   [5] Laws 1890, c. 116; Laws 1893, c. 95.

kota,[1] Texas,[2] and Wyoming,[3] and provide for the appointment by the Governor of officers called, very commonly, Public Examiners or Examiners of Accounts, whose duties are to formulate methods of keeping accounts to be adopted by the financial officers of the counties, and in some cases by those of the cities, to examine the accounts of such officers at least once a year, and to report to the Governor the results of their work. These laws usually vest ample powers in the Public Examiners to enable them to get at the truth, and punish severely all attempts to hinder them in their work.[4]

Finally, it is to be remembered that in times past the legislature has in more than one instance voluntarily divested itself, or been deprived by the constitution, of powers for whose exercise it had proved itself unfit. Up to the present time its mantle has, in these cases, fallen upon the courts rather than upon the administration. Thus the whole matter of divorce, formerly attended to by the legislature by the passage of special acts, has

---

[1] Laws 1887, c. 124. [2] Laws 1891, c. 69.
[3] Laws 1890-91, c. 84.
[4] Among the recommendations of the Fassett Committee, whose report has several times already been referred to, we find a bill providing uniform methods of accounting and imposing upon all cities, within the state of New York, the duty to file their accounts annually with the Governor of the state.

been put into the hands of the courts, subject to the obligation to act in accordance with general laws passed upon the subject by the legislature. In the same way the matter of claims against the government, which were paid formerly in accordance with special acts passed by the legislature, has, in the case of the Federal government and in several instances in the case of the state governments, been put into the jurisdiction of either special courts established for the purpose, or into that of the ordinary courts.[1]

It will be seen thus that the power of the legislature to regulate matters by special act has been either taken from it by the people or voluntarily given up by it in more than one instance in our past history, where it was proven that such special acts were improper. It will be seen also that a central administrative control over various matters of administrative importance affecting the state as a whole, has been developed in our state system of government for quite a time, and has begun to develop over certain of our municipal corporations in several of the states. We are therefore justified in expecting that this central administrative control over municipal corporations will, notwithstanding that it may be regarded at first blush

---

[1] See King, "Claims against Governments" in *The American Law Register and Review*, November, 1893.

as quite contrary to our historic and fundamental principle of local self-government or administration, be given a much wider development just so soon as the people of the country become convinced of the unwisdom of our present system of legislative control of local municipal matters. When that time comes, and it would appear now as if it must surely come soon, the retention of our present method of legislative control will be unnecessary, and the demand for greater powers of municipal home rule may be satisfied without danger of disintegration and of the sacrifice of the interests of the state as a whole.

Of course, it will readily be admitted that the delimitation of a sphere of municipal autonomy and the exclusion of the state legislature from action within it are not the only means of solving the problem of municipal government. Proper organization of municipal institutions, selection of competent and upright municipal officers, and civic patriotism are all necessary. But it is believed that little progress in municipal government reform can be made until it is known what the sphere of municipal government is, and until an ample degree of local autonomy in that sphere is secured.

INDEX

Administration, *see* Local administration.

Administrative control over municipalities, in England, 234 *et seq.*; on the continent, 251 *et seq.*; necessity of in United States, 264 *et seq.*

Administrative courts, in France, 116; in United States, 270.

Administrative law in the United States, tendency of, 181.

Administrative organization of municipal corporation, interference with by legislature, 223.

Aldermen, *see* Municipal council.

Alienation of municipal property, 107, 209-220, 227.

American administration law, tendency of, 181.

American cities, *see* City in United States.

American local administration, *see* Local administration in United States.

Appointment, power of, an executive act, 90.

Aqueduct commission in New York city, 22.

Assessments, special, legislative control over, 85, 86, 89, 225; power of, not to be implied, 51, 225.

Bonds, municipal, execution of judgment against, 227; implied power to issue, doubtful, 51; legislative authorization to issue, 52, 86; legislative power over the issue of, 86; money raised by, a public trust, 192.

Borough in England, history of, to 19th century, 12; incorporation of, 99, 101. (*See* Local administration.)

Borough in United States, *see* Cities and Villages.

Boundaries of city, effect of change of, 188, 193, 194; not to be changed by special act, 81, 222.

Bounties, military, reimbursement of municipal corporation for, 204.

Bridges, liability of municipal corporations for management of, 160, 176.

Brooklyn, experience of Hon. Seth Low as mayor of, 22.

Bryce, Hon. James, quoted, on Supreme Court, 33.

Canon law, influence of on legal development, 13.

Cemeteries, liability of municipal corporations for management of, 152; transfer of, to private corporation, 97.

Central administrative control over cities, in England, 234 *et seq.*; on the continent, 251 *et seq.*; need of, in United States, 264 *et seq.*

Charters, *see* Municipal charters.

Church in Middle Ages, govern-

274 INDEX

mental functions of, 38, a *quasi*-public corporation, 38.
City council, *see* Municipal council.
City courts in United States, outgrowths of city council, 3.
City departments, *see* Finance, Parks, etc.
City, *see* Municipal corporations and Local administration.
City in England, history of, to 19th century, 12.
City in United States, history of, 2-5; lack of civic patriotism in, 8; need of local autonomy in, 9, 29; public character of, 18, 53.
Civic patriotism, lack of, in American cities, 8.
Civil liberty in United States, disadvantages of method of securing, 86; guaranteed by the constitution, 35.
Civil liberty, how delimited in other states, 35; protection of, by English Parliament, 42; sphere of, varies, 36.
Classification of municipal corporations, principles of, 65-77, 263.
College, presence of, a basis of municipal classification, 67.
Commissions, municipal, delegation of taxing power to, 25; English, in 18th century, 15; general law affecting, 68; forbidden by state constitutions, 60; in New York city, 22; Philadelphia City Hall, 25.
Consolidated Municipal Corporations Act of 1882, in England, 240.
Constitution of United States, civil liberty in, 35; interpreted by Supreme Court, 33; private property protected by, 102; sovereignty in, 34.
Constitutional limitations of power of the legislature over municipalities, 56 *et seq.*, 92; effect of, 62.
Contracts, liability of state for, 180-183; municipal charters not, 31; power of municipal corporation to make, 228; *see* Property rights of municipal corporations, 184 *et seq.*
Corporate authorities, definition of, 83.
Corporate powers, defined, 82 *et seq.*
Corporations, liability of, for torts of officers, 116; private, aid of, not a municipal function, 105; private, charter of, a contract, 40; private right of, to use streets, 61; private, sphere of action of, 38, 39; private, status affected by state constitutions, 40; *see* Municipal corporations.
Council, city, *see* Municipal council.
County in England, incorporation of, 99; *see* Local administration.
County in United States, classification of, by population, 71, 72; division of, by special act forbidden, 61; judicial administration, a function of, 79; internal affairs of, 81; internal affairs of, protected from legislative interference by state constitutions, 59; property rights of, protected by courts, 186 *et seq.*; liability of, for management of property, 153, 161. (*See Quasi*-municipal corporations.)
Courts, control of, over municipal affairs, 261 *et seq.*; effect of constitutional control of, on responsibility of legislature, 41; inability of, to correct evils in municipal government, 30, 55; interpretation of municipal pow-

ers, 46; protection of people of municipal corporation by, 208 *et seq.*; protection of property rights of municipal corporations by, 184 *et seq.*

Courts, control of, over administration, in England, 34; in France and Germany, 116; in United States, 181.

Criminal administration, liability of municipal corporation for, 139, 140.

Delegation of legislative powers, *see* Legislature.

Delimitation of the sphere of private action of municipal corporations, 101 *et seq.*

Democracy, applied to municipal government, 3.

Departments, *see* Municipal departments.

Easements, natural, liability of government for disturbance of, 115.

Economic conditions, influence of, on municipal life, 93; on municipal government in England, 12.

Education, *see* Public school administration.

Election to municipal office, in early England, 12.

Electric lighting, 47. (*See* Lighting.)

Enumerated powers, rule of, applied to municipal corporations, 45.

Excise administration, action of English Parliament, 1888, 42; classification of cities for, 67; compensation to dealers in England, 1888, 42; legislative control over, in New York city, 22.

Execution of judgment against municipal corporation, *see* Judgment.

Fassett Committee, report of, 23, 28.

Ferries, *see* Wharves.

Feudal system, influence on municipal corporations, 109, 251.

Financial administration, borrowing money, *see* Indebtedness; of municipalities, borrowing money, *see* Indebtedness; central control of, 269; common-law powers of, 50; extent of delegated powers of, 52; issue of bonds, *see* Bonds; legal rules of, 225; power of legislatures over, 26. (*See* Taxation, Bonds, etc.)

Fire administration, appointment of, by legislature, 90; liability of municipal corporation for negligence in, 119, 121, 123, 137, 138, 171, 174–176.

Fire department, legislative control over, in New York city, 22.

Franchises, grant of, by special act forbidden, 61; of ferries, 201.

Franchises, street, legislative authorization of grant of, necessary, 144; legislative control over, 207.

Frederick the Great, influence of, on Prussian local administration, 255.

Frederick William I., influence of, on Prussian local administration, 255.

French local administration, *see* Local administration.

French Revolution, influence of, on local government, 252.

Gas-works, liability of municipal corporations for management of, 153; a municipal purpose, 141; use of streets for, 144, 147.

General laws required, for incorporation of municipalities, 58. (*See* Special acts.)

German cities, early, 11.

Geographical conditions, not a

basis of municipal classification, 74; influence of, on municipal life, 93; interference of legislation with, 222.
Government, liability of, for torts of officers, 112; the representative of the sovereign, 113, 180.
Governmental powers, distinguished from corporate, 80.

Health of cities, *see* Sanitary administration.
Highways, distinguished from streets, 146; liability of *quasi*-municipal corporations for management of, 163, 173 *et seq.*; liability of municipal corporations for, *see* Streets.
Home rule, European method of, 233.
Home rule for American cities, absence of, 8; not attainable under rule of enumerated powers, 93; encroachment of legislature on domain of, 54; judicial basis of, 84–86; methods to ensure, 259 *et seq.*; need of, 9; New York constitutional amendment, 66; power to frame charters granted by state constitutions, 61; sphere of, undetermined, 10. (*See* Private action.)
Hospital administration, liability of city for, 139, 140, 161, 166; property of, protected by the courts, 199.

Implied powers of municipality, rule of, 45, 48.
Incorporation, *see* Municipal charters.
Indebtedness, municipal, lack of control over, 29; implied powers to incur, 51; power to incur, delegated to commission, 25. (*See* Bonds.)

Individual freedom, necessity for, 37.
Internal affairs, definition of, 78 *et seq.*; judicial construction of special act affecting, 74; legislature forbidden by state constitution to regulate, 59.
Interference of legislature with municipalities, *see* Legislative interference.

Judgment, execution of, against municipal property, 213–220; not an incumbrance on municipal property, 217; nor a lien on real estate, 217.
Judicial administration a function of counties, 79.
Judicial control over administration, in England, 34; in United States, 181.
Judicial control over municipal affairs, 261 *et seq.*
Judicial control, *see* Courts and Control over administration.
Judicial duties of municipalities, distinguished from ministerial, 141.
Judgment, execution of, against municipal corporation, 213–220, 227.
Judges, municipal officers created, in American colonies, 16.
Justices of the peace, municipal officers, constituted such by charter, 16.
Legal conditions of American cities, effect of, on local government, 8 *et seq.*
Legislation, special, *see* Special acts.
Legislative control over municipalities, appointment of officers, 90; causes of, 43; effect of, 28; constitutional limitations on, 56 *et seq.*; effect of constitutional

limitations on, 61; extent of, 17, 230; financial, 26, 225; internal affairs, 59; judicial administration, 79; necessity of, 45, 53, 94, 100, 259; New York city, 23 *et seq.*; officers, 23, 71, 84-90, 223; parks, 83, 84, 90; Philadelphia, 25; police, 21, 79, 85, 90, 208; private rights, 101; property rights, 186 *et seq.*, 226; sanitary administration, 22, 79; special assessments, 51, 85, 86; sphere of, undetermined, 9, 19, 32, 221; taxation, 60, 82, 86, 102; streets, 142-149.

Legislative interference in municipal affairs in United States, cause of, 8, 233; effect of, 8, 28; extent of, 19; forbidden by state constitutions, 56; limits of, 222 *et seq.*; in New York, 20, 23 *et seq.*, 54; partisan political reasons for, 26; remedy for, 9, 259 *et seq.* (*See* Legislative control.)

Legislative powers, municipal corporations, not liable for non-exercise of, 118, 123.

Legislature, classification of municipal corporations by, 65; constitutional limitations of the power of, over municipal affairs, 56 *et seq.*; effect of constitutional provisions on responsibility of, 41; encroachment on field of local government, 54; importance of in American administration, 18, 185; local powers of, in United States, 24. (*See* Legislative control, etc.)

Liability of municipal corporations, for management of property, 150 *et seq.*; for torts, 111 *et seq.*, 180-182.

Libraries, a municipal purpose, 199.

Licenses, implied power of municipalities to derive revenue from, 51; liability of city for, 125, 136.

Lighting, early English administration of, 14. (*See* Gas-works.)

Liquor laws, *see* Excise administration.

Local administration in England, compared with American, 248; history of, to 19th century, 12; inconveniences of old system of, 101, *note* 4; influence of continental ideas on, 109; judicial control of, 34; local autonomy in, 250, 266; modern development of, 234 *et seq.*; powers of Local Government Board, 237, 248; reforms of 1835, 8, 244; acts of 1882 and 1888, 42, 100, 240; act of 1894, 247; theory of, 99.

Local administration in France, centralization of, 254; Communes Act of 1884, 254; election of officers, 256; financial, 257; municipal councils, 256; origin of, 251; police, 257; sanitary, 257.

Local administration in Prussia, Act of 1808, 254; centralization of, 255; election of officers, 256; financial, 257; municipal councils, 256; origin of, 25; police, 257; public school, 257; sanitary, 257.

Local administration in United States, development of, 100; effect of confusing private rights and public privileges, on, 41; a function of local self-government, 84-86; inefficiency and extravagance of, 2; influence of continental ideas on, 109; lack of concentration in, 259; lack of local autonomy, 8, 99 *et seq.*; sphere of legislative control over, undetermined, 9, 19,

32, 221. (*See* Municipal corporations, Officers, etc.)
Local consent required to special laws, 58.
Local government, in England, 234-250; continental methods, 251-258; administrative control over, in United States, 264 *et seq.* (*See* Local administration, Legislative control.)
Local government act of 1888, English, 42, 100, 240.
Local government board in England, powers of, over localities, 237, 248.
Local officers, *see* Officers.

Mandamus, to enforce execution of judgment against municipality, 213.
Markets, a municipal purpose, 141; liability of municipal corporations for management of, 153; property in, protected by the courts, 199; property in, when subject to execution, 220.
Material powers of municipalities, 49.
Mayor in England, chosen by the council, 4.
Mayor in France, tenure of, at will of central government, 256.
Mayor in United States, early position of, 2; justice of the peace in colonial times, 16; originally elected by city council, 4; powers of, increasing of late, 5; not a state officer, 87.
Metropolitan police district, in New York, 21.
Ministerial duties of municipalities, distinguished from judicial, 141.
Mortgage of municipal property, 227. (*See* Alienation.)
Municipal affairs, defined, 77 *et seq.*, 221; in relation to liability of municipal corporations for management of property, 150 *et seq.*; in relation to liability of municipal corporations for torts, 111 *et seq.*
Municipal bonds, *see* Bonds.
Municipal borough in England, history of, to 19th century, 12; incorporation of, 99, 101. (*See* Municipal corporations, Local administration, in England.)
Municipal charter in England, earliest instance of, 12; effect of, 13; incorporation of boroughs, 99, 101; movement against, under the Stuarts, 243; purpose of, 13.
Municipal charter in United States, amendment of, forbidden by state constitutions, 57; not a contract, 31; effect of, 101; general laws required for granting, by state constitutions, 58; judicial construction of, 46 *et seq.*; legal position of, 31; original source of, 47; power to frame, granted to cities by state constitutions, 61, 66, 81, 93; protection of private rights vested under, 184 *et seq.*; special acts granting, forbidden by state constitutions, 56.
Municipal commissions, *see* Commissions.
Municipal corporations, origin of, 11.
Municipal corporation in England, early history of, 12; influence of Anglo-Norman ideas on, 109; liability of, for torts of officers, 116 *et seq.*; members of, in early times, 13; prostitution of, 13, 242; reform of 1835, 8, 244; acts of 1882, and 1888, 42, 100, 240. (*See* Municipal charter and Local legislation.)
Municipal corporation in France,

rule of enumerated restrictions applied to, 253; local autonomy of, 253. (*See* Local administration in France.)
Municipal corporation in Prussia, general powers of, 253; local autonomy of, 253; reform of 1808, 254. (*See* Local administration in Prussia.)
Municipal corporation in United States, alienation of property of, 107, 209 *et seq.*; agents of state government, 18, 94, 140, 143, 191; classification of, by legislature, 65–77; classification of, limited by state constitutions, 92; compared with English, 100; constituted a trustee, 188–191; contractual powers of, 228; corporate and governmental powers of, distinguished, 80; delimitation of sphere of private action of, 101 *et seq.*; double nature of, 18, 40, 101; early history of, 2–5; effect of constitutional guarantees on, 62; powers of, enumerated, 45, 47; failure of, to enforce ordinances, 118 *et seq.*; incorporation of, by special act forbidden by state constitutions, 56; liability of, for management of property, 150 *et seq.*; liability of, for torts, 111 *et seq.*, 228; not liable for exercise of legislative powers, 118; origin of, 15; organ of central government, 17; powers of, 45, 111, 118; private capacity of, 141, 221; private liabilities of, 106, 111; property rights of, 50, 101 *et seq.*, 184 *et seq.*, 226; private rights of, 43, 101, 111; *quasi*-private nature of, 108, 141; sphere of private action of, 221 *et seq.*
Municipal council in England, 2, 4, 242.
Municipal council in France, 256.
Municipal council in Prussia, 256.
Municipal council in United States, development of, 3; election of, 4; judicial functions of, 3, 16; original form of, 2.
Municipal debts, *see* Indebtedness.
Municipal departments in United States, heads of, originally appointed by city council, 4; elected by people, 4. (*See* Finance, Fire administration, etc.)
Municipal finance, *see* Financial administration.
Municipal government, *see* City, Local administration, etc.
Municipal officers, *see* Officers.
Municipal paving, *see* Paving.
Municipal property, protection of, 102.
Municipal taxation, *see* Taxation.

Name, not a basis of municipal classification, 74.
Negligence, liability of government for, 115.
New York constitutional amendment, 1894, provisions of, 97; criticism of, 266.
New York city, history of legislative control over, 20 *et seq.*; powers of officers of, under original charter, 16; public character of, 53.
Nuisance, liability of government for, 115; liability of municipal corporations for, 120, 125.

Officers, municipal, in England, compensated by Parliament in 1888, 42; election of, in early times, 12; powers of, 234 *et seq.*
Officers, municipal, in France, 256.
Officers, municipal, in Prussia, 256.
Officers, municipal, in United States, acts of, *ultra vires*, void, 46; agents of central govern-

ment, 17, 224; constituted justices of the peace in American colonies, 16; definition of, 82 *et seq.*; duties of, 18; duties of, not to be regulated by special act, 81, 224; distinguished from state officers, 87 *et seq.*, 224; effect of legislative interference on, 29; liability of corporation for torts of, 112 *et seq.*; popular election of, guaranteed by state constitution, 60; power of legislature over, 23, 71, 84, 88, 90, 223, 224; salaries of, fixed by legislature, 22; salaries of, not to be regulated by special act, 81, 82, 224; special act discharging, 71.

Ordinances, municipal, not contracts, 120; force of, 135; liability for non-enforcement of, 118 *et seq.*; suspension of, 121.

Parish in England, highway duties of, enforced by public remedies, 109; increase of functions of, 14; organized under the Tudors, 15. (*See* Local administration.)

Parish in United States, *see* Quasi-municipal corporation.

Park administration, alienation of property of, 210; control of legislature over, 83, 84, 90, 199, 203; a corporate purpose, 83, 84; property protected by the courts, 199, 210.

Parliament, English, control of courts over acts of, 34; relation to civil liberty, 42.

Party, influence of, in municipal affairs, 26.

Pauperism, *see* Poor-law administration.

Paving, early English administration of, 14; in New York, legislative control over, 23. (*See* Streets.)

Personal property, alienation of, by municipal corporation, 213.

Philadelphia, City Hall of, 25; powers of officers under original charter, 16.

Police administration, character of local officers of, 88; a function of central government, 79-90, 134, 223; liability for torts of officers of, 135, 136; negligence of officers of, 135, 136, 172; officers of, agents of central government, 88, 224; status of officers of, 88; in England, 239; in France, 257; in Prussia, 257.

Police power, in early American municipalities, 15, 16; in early English municipalities, 16; extent of, 261; exercise of, a public duty, 133; powers to be implied from, 48, 49; too wide in American states, 37.

Police, metropolitan police district in New York, 21.

Political influence, power of, in municipal affairs, 27.

Poor-law administration, under Church in Middle Ages, 38; early English, centralized, 14; English system of, 234-239; liability of municipal corporation for, 139, 140, 158; localized in American cities, 18.

Poor-Law Amendment Act of 1834, English, 234.

Population, a basis of municipal classification, 68-76.

Private action of municipal corporation, in American law, 221 *et seq.*; means of delimiting sphere of, 99 *et seq.*

Private corporations, *see* Corporations.

Private rights, confused with public privileges, 39; protected by the courts, 41, 222. (*See* Civil liberty.)

Private rights of municipal corporation in property, protected, 184 *et seq.*

Property of municipal corporation, alienation of, 107, 209 *et seq.;* control of legislature over, 226; force of judicial decisions on, 222; liability for management of, 142, 150 *et seq.;* protected by constitutional provision, 102, 184 *et seq.;* subject to taxation, 217.

Property, private, duty to protect, implied from police power, 48.

Public privileges, confused with private rights, 40.

Public school administration, under Church in Middle Ages, 38.

Public school administration in England, centralized in early times, 14; modern development of, 236–238.

Public school administration in Prussia, 257.

Public school administration in United States, liability of municipal corporations for, 154–158, 164–166, 169; localized, 18; a municipal function, 78; property of, exempt from execution, 215; property of, protected by the courts, 205–207.

Publicity, lack of, in municipal matters, 29; secured by New York constitution, 98.

Public works, a corporate purpose, 81, 84, 85; liability of municipal corporations in construction of, 127–133, 141, 176; officers of, municipal, 88, 224; *quasi*-private character of, 141. (*See* Property, Water works, etc.)

Quasi-municipal corporation, alienation of personal property of, 113 *et seq.;* liability of, for management of property, 154–180;
private property, rights of, 184 *et seq.;* doubtful status of, 58.

Quasi-private nature of municipal corporations, 108, 141.

Quo warranto, against cities in England, under the Stuarts, 243.

Railroads, alienation of stock held by municipality, 213; power of municipality to buy stock of, 104.

Railroads, street, municipal revenues from, subject to execution, 218; use of street for, 61, 144, 147, 207.

Recorder in United States, colonial position of, 16.

Reformation, influence of, on functions of government, 14.

"Rings," cause of, in first half of century, 4.

Riot, liability of city for, 135.

Roman law, idea of corporate, capacity of, 110; municipalities of, 11.

Salaries of officers, compensation for loss of, in England, 42; not to be regulated by special act, 81, 82, 224.

Sanitary administration in England, centralized, 14; modern development, 236.

Sanitary administration in France, 257. [257.

Sanitary administration in Prussia.

Sanitary administration in United States, central administrative control in New York, 268; a function of central government, 79, 95, 224; implied from police power, 48; legislative control over, 22, 79, 89, 223; liability of municipal corporation for negligence of officers, 137; localized, 18; officers of, agents of central government, 224.

Schools, *see* Public school administration.

School districts, doubtful status of, as *quasi*-municipal corporations, 58; liability of, for management of property, 154–158, 169.

Senate committee's report, New York, 23, 28.

Sewers, liability of municipal corporation in construction of, 125–133; a *quasi*-private municipal purpose, 141.

Social conditions, influence of, on municipal government, in England, 12; in United States, 7, 93.

Sovereign government, the representative of, 113, 180; liability of, for torts of officers, 116.

Sovereignty in American system, 34; in English system, 34; in municipal corporations, 111.

Special act of legislature, definition of, 63 *et seq.*, 91; defined by New York constitution, 97; English definition of, 250; concerning financial matters, 225; judicial interpretation of, 63 *et seq.*; concerning officers, 223. (*See* Private municipal action.)

Special act of legislature forbidden by state constitutions amending charters, 57; appointing local commissions, 60; conferring corporate powers, 58; creating local offices, 60; dividing counties or changing county seats, 61; futility of such provisions, 94; granting street franchise, 61; imposing taxes for local purposes, 60; incorporating cities and villages, 56; opening or vacating streets or highways, 61; regulating internal affairs of counties and towns, 59.

Special assessments, *see* Assessments.

Special legislation, *see* Private municipal action, Special act.

Special legislation, municipal, absence of, in Germany and France, 257.

Spheres of private municipal action in American law, 221 *et seq.*

Spoils system in American cities, 6.

State, corporate capacity of, 114, 180; relation of, to civil liberty, 37; a subject of private law in France and Germany, 116.

Stein, Baron, influence of, on Prussian local administration, 254.

Streets, alienation of property in, 211; control of legislature over, 90, 142–149, 207; distinguished from highways, 146; franchises of, granting of, by special act forbidden, 61; liability of municipal corporations for management of, 125–127, 142–149, 172, 176, 228; lighting of, 47; nuisances licensed in, 125–127; officers of, not agents of central government, 224; opening, or vacating of, by special act, forbidden, 61; property rights of municipal corporation in, 142–149, 228; use of, for public works, 144.

Street railroads, *see* Railroads.

Suffrage, municipal, universal manhood, 4.

Supreme Court of United States, doctrine of, on civil liberty, 37; functions of, 33; protection of property rights of municipal corporations by, 186.

Taxation, local, central administrative control of, 268; local, colonial conditions, 16; in early English cities, 12; effect of inequality of, in cities, 95; exercise of powers of, 225; imposition by special act for corporate purpose, forbidden, 60, 82, 86; legislative power to impose, 101, 221; money raised by, a trust fund, 192, 205, 227; money derived by, not subject to execution, 214; power of, granted to commission, 25; effect of relinquishing power of, 39; power must be expressly granted, 50, 225; present rule of, 17; purposes of, 78, 102; rate may be limited, 51; transfer of money raised by, 205; private municipal property, subject to, 218.

Torts, liability of government for, enumeration of liabilities, 115; in France, 116, 181; in Germany, 116, 181; in United States, 112-117, 180-182; municipal corporations in United States, 111 *et seq.*, 228.

Town, internal affairs of, protected from legislative interference by state constitutions, 59; liability of, for management of property, 153 *et seq.*; property rights of, protected by courts, 186 *et seq.* (See *Quasi*-municipal corporation.)

Township, *see* Town.

Transportation, in New York, legislative control over, 23.

Trespass, liability of government for, 115, 132; municipal corporation for, 168.

Trustee, municipal corporation made, 188-191, 193.

Ultra vires, acts of municipal officers, void, 46.

Veto, suspensive, given to municipal corporations in New York, 66.

Village in United States, charter of, *see* Municipal charters; corporate powers of, *see* Municipal corporations.

Water works, liability of municipal corporations for management of, 152; a municipal purpose, 141; officers of, not agents of central government, 224; private property of municipal corporation, 199, 203, 220; municipal, subject to taxation, 218; property in, exempt from execution, 216, 218; use of streets for, 144, 147.

Wharves, alienation of, 212; liability of municipal corporations for management of, 152; a municipal purpose, 141; property rights in, protected by the courts, 195, 200-202.

www.ingramcontent.com/pod-product-compliance
Lightning Source LLC
Chambersburg PA
CBHW022103230426
43672CB00008B/1267